The American Market of the Future

THE CHARLES C. MOSKOWITZ LECTURES   NUMBER VI

ARNO H. JOHNSON

VICE PRESIDENT AND SENIOR ECONOMIST
J. WALTER THOMPSON COMPANY

GILBERT E. JONES

PRESIDENT
IBM WORLD TRADE CORPORATION

DARRELL B. LUCAS

PROFESSOR OF MARKETING AND
CHAIRMAN OF THE DEPARTMENT
NEW YORK UNIVERSITY

The American Market

of the Future

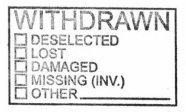
THE CHARLES C. MOSKOWITZ LECTURES
SCHOOL OF COMMERCE
NEW YORK UNIVERSITY

© *1966 by New York University*
Library of Congress Catalog Card Number: 66-22222
Manufactured in the United States of America
Distributed by New York University Press

SECOND PRINTING 1967

THE HEALTH AND CHARACTER of the American economy are profoundly affected by the level and composition of demand. For example, trends in unemployment and price levels are closely related to total effective demand, while policy decisions vital to the future of the nation hinge on analysis of the relationships. Equally important to the nation is the composition of demand and changes in it. It is one of the central features of our market system that the kinds of goods and services produced reflect the wants of our people, freely expressed through their voluntarily taken spending decisions. Of course these decisions reflect the character of our civilization, as they are reflected in turn in the quality and tone of our standard of living.

Centering on the theme, "The American Market of the Future," the 1965 Moskowitz lecture series dealt with various aspects of the foregoing matters. Arno H. Johnson, Vice-President and Senior Economist of the

J. Walter Thompson Company, as well as an outstanding person in the field of marketing research, concerned himself with the potential upgrading of consumer living standards, and the relationship of such upgrading to economic growth and well-being a decade hence. Mr. Johnson's lecture will linger long in the memory of his audience because of its tone of carefully confident optimism, which he managed to transmit in the midst of the deep darkness brought by the great power failure of November 9, 1965.

Gilbert E. Jones, President of the IBM World Trade Corporation and a leading executive with experience in the increasingly important area of international markets, discussed "The Changing International Market and its Challenges to the United States." Emphasizing the rapid rate at which our world is becoming ever more closely interconnected and interdependent, he saw unparalleled opportunities for America's industrial society in helping to meet the burgeoning demands abroad for vastly increased amounts of goods. Mr. Jones' optimism was enthusiastic and infectious.

Darrell B. Lucas, Chairman of the Department of Marketing of the Schools of Business of New York University, and careful researcher into and authority on consumer psychology, considered "Consumer Patterns in the 1975 Market." Assuming continued economic growth in the United States, Professor Lucas foresaw so affluent a level of income in 1975 as to significantly challenge the marketing experts of our nation in their efforts to stimulate the wants of America's consumers. He spoke also of the effort which will be necessary to educate affluent consumers to new and qualitatively better wants. Looking to the underdeveloped and non-industrialized nations of the world, Dr. Lucas raised significant questions as to the probability of their enjoying a significant advancement in consumption in the next decade. In this regard his talk was somewhat sobering to his listeners.

The School of Commerce is honored to have sponsored these stimulating lectures and to offer the authoritative views of these distinguished experts.

Abraham L. Gitlow,
ACTING DEAN
SCHOOL OF COMMERCE
NEW YORK UNIVERSITY

February, 1966

THE CHARLES C. MOSKOWITZ LECTURES

THE CHARLES C. MOSKOWITZ LECTURES were established through the generosity of a distinguished alumnus of the School of Commerce, Mr. Charles C. Moskowitz of the Class of 1914, who retired after many years as Vice President-Treasurer and a director of Loew's Inc.

Mr. Moskowitz's aim in establishing the lectures was to contribute to the understanding of the function of business and its related disciplines in society, by providing a public forum for the dissemination of enlightened business theories and practices.

The School of Commerce and New York University are deeply grateful to Mr. Moskowitz for his continued interest in, and contribution to, the education and public-service program of his alma mater.

CONTENTS

xi

THE FRAMEWORK OF AMERICAN MARKETS IN 1975

by Arno H. Johnson

VICE PRESIDENT AND SENIOR ECONOMIST

J. WALTER THOMPSON COMPANY

THE FRAMEWORK of American markets in 1975 is being shaped right now by the rapid and dynamic changes evident in the whole social and economic structure of the United States as well as of other areas in the free world. Indications are that these changes will accelerate in the next decade and that there will be an opportunity for a major worldwide upsurge in consumer standards of living and education as productivity per capita mounts.

Businessmen and marketing men in particular should be aware of these trends since it is the *consumer* and the potential *upgrading* of his *standard of living* that is fast becoming the real key to economic growth.

There are seven factors of dynamic change in the United States which should be watched closely in developing plans for the next decade. To varying degrees, these changes in the United States may be forecasting similar trends in other world markets. These factors are:

1   There is an insistent pressure for economic growth in the United States — enough to provide 20 million more non-agricultural jobs by 1975 (from 68 million to 88 million). $215 billion of additional purchases of goods and services annually by consumers (from $425 billion to $640 billion) will be needed to provide jobs for the larger, better educated, and more productive labor force — a labor force capable of producing a *trillion dollar economy by 1975!*

The economy of the United States faces the task of expanding the demand for goods and services to justify the creation of *2 million* more non-agricultural job opportunities each year during the next decade — a rate that is more than twice the annual average of 1950 to 1965. This expansion will call for a substantial and voluntary upgrading of living standards.

2   A movement upward in income groups, brought about by economic growth and increased productivity, is giving mass millions of the United States population greater discretionary spending power and latitude in the upgrading of their way of life. As a result, old saturation points for marketing various goods and services have already become obsolete, and consumer attitudes and desires will become increasingly important in determining new ones.

3   A rapid rise in the educational level of the population of the United States is influencing health, personal care, and home interests and is causing accelerated changes in consumer needs. Habits change

with a heightened exposure to books, magazines, newspapers, educational materials, and television.

4   Markets respond to new trends in the population. Continued growth and shifts in the age distribution of the population are affecting housing needs, the labor force, as well as medical and personal care requirements. The growing number of adolescents, of young housewives learning to shop and prepare for family daily needs, and of persons over sixty-five represent increases in very different consumer requirements.

The fact that the number of families with two or more children has increased substantially is evidence of a trend toward a family-oriented way of life. And the number of United States households is expected to expand at the average rate of 1.3 million annually, rather than 900,000 as in the past 15 years, to a total of 70 million.

5   There have been startling changes in the composition of the labor force in the United States — less manual labor, increased numbers of skilled workers, and an increase in the number of married women workers. With married women continuing to expand the labor force and family income there is a consequent need for convenience and labor-saving devices in the home; and with education and automation exerting still further pressure for greater skills in the labor force, the composition of markets could change drastically.

6   The population has shown a general shift in residence from the core of the city to nearby suburbs. A

rapid decline in farm population has been accompanied by spectacular increases in farm productivity per man hour. These changes are causing a revolution in housing needs as well as in the distribution of goods which is manifesting itself in the rapid growth of self-service supermarkets and drug stores, discount outlets, and shopping centers.

7   The expansion of competitive efforts to change people's buying habits has been an increasingly important factor in the trend toward better living standards and economic growth. Eighty-six percent of the growth of advertising in the last century took place in the twenty-five years since 1940 — and this accounts also for 84 percent of the total growth in standards of living as measured by personal consumption expenditures.

The total expenditure for advertising in the United States may more than double by the end of the next decade compared with the estimated $15 billion for 1965. This could be the essential ingredient in sufficiently increasing consumer demands to provide markets necessary for the trillion-dollar productive ability expected by 1975–1976.

The following discussion of trends and pressures in the United States will indicate that the decade starting in 1966 will offer opportunities for substantial economic growth and a rapid upsurge in living standards that may have a worldwide impact. Similar trends are already becoming increasingly apparent in many nations.

Actually, an analysis of the potential improvement in

living standards in just two areas of the free world — Western Europe and the United States — indicates that a conservative estimate of additional consumer demands for goods and services in the next ten years exceeds $400 billion. The velocity of this estimated change in consumption is emphasized by the fact that, as recently as 1950, the total personal consumption of these same areas (in constant dollars) was only $303 billion. Hence, the potential addition to markets through the upgrading of the total standard of living in these two areas in the next ten years alone far surpasses the total growth of Western Europe and the United States in all history up to 1950.

Very little attention has been paid to the fact that the productivity of a nation's people cannot be stimulated and utilized without upgrading the standard of living and expanding the sales of goods and services to match production and thus provide employment and income commensurate with the improved productive ability.

Nor have we fully recognized that expansion and improvement of plant and equipment, and interest in private investment, depend ultimately on *growth in consumption.* Industry cannot continue to invest in expansion or improvement or in research and development of new products and services without soundly based estimates of increased *demand* for its products and an environment of *profit potential* in the sale of these products.

In the past, *investment in the creation of consumer demand* (i.e., advertising and public relations efforts) has not been keeping pace with *investment in new plant and equipment.* Hence, consumer demand has not been growing as rapidly as it should to meet the expanded productive capacity or increased production efficiency implied by new plant and equipment expenditures.

Because there must be a logical relationship between investment in new plant and equipment and anticipated consumer sales, one might reasonably expect that as there are increases in plant investment there should be corresponding increases in investment in consumer franchise. There is only one way that plant investments can be amortized and that is through sales and profits. Yet, during the past six years, the rate of total investment in new plant and equipment has increased 63 percent (from $32.54 billion to $52.95 in 1965, fourth quarter) and investment in new *manufacturing* plant and equipment, 92 percent (from $12 billion to $23 billion), while the increase in advertising volume during the same period has been only 36 percent (from $11 billion in 1959 to an estimated $15 billion in 1965). And total personal consumption has increased only 36 percent from $311.2 billion to an estimated $425 billion in 1965. This is *less than half* the rate of growth in expenditures for new plant and equipment in manufacturing.

This rapidly expanding capacity to produce and the consequent pressure for employment should revolutionize our ideas about needed increases in *consumer demand* and the amount of investment in public relations, advertising and selling effort needed to educate, encourage, and stimulate that consumer demand.

Accelerated Economic Growth for New Jobs

One basic fact underlies the discussions of need for and stimulation of greater economic growth in America. By 1975 the American public will be demanding *20 million more* non-agricultural jobs at much higher levels of productivity (*See* Chart No. 1). The needed growth from 68 million non-agricultural employment in the fall of 1965 to at least 88 million by 1975 means we face the task of creating an average of two million net new job opportunities each year during the next decade. That is *twice* the rate of annual increase of the last 15 years. During 1965, with an increase of 2.1 million (September 1965 versus September 1964), we have reached the level of annual growth in employment needed to stem unemployment and assure adequate economic growth. But we must maintain at least that annual rate of growth for the whole of the next decade!

With 98 million expected in the total labor force by 1975 and with a continued decline in agricultural employment to about 3½ million and with an arbitrary estimate of 2½ million needed for the Armed Forces, 20 million more non-agricultural jobs will be needed by 1975 to keep unemployment down to a level around four million. And these new workers will be better educated and capable of greater productivity.

Providing these 20 million jobs will require substantially expanded sales of goods and services. It will require increases of demand and markets in a proportion far greater than the population growth itself and

Chart 1
U.S. NEEDS 20 MILLION NEW NON-AGRICULTURAL JOBS BY 1975

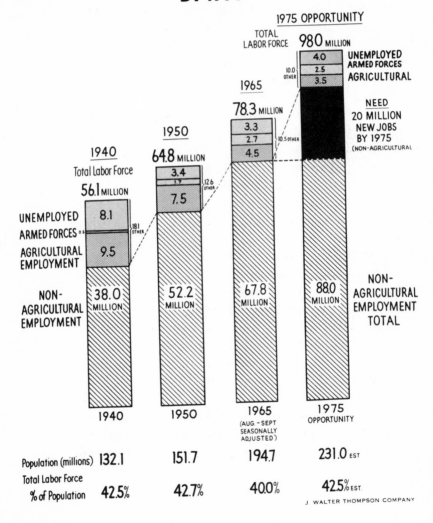

	1940	1950	1965 (AUG.-SEPT. SEASONALLY ADJUSTED)	1975 OPPORTUNITY
Population (millions)	132.1	151.7	194.7	231.0 EST
Total Labor Force % of Population	42.5%	42.7%	40.0%	42.5% EST.

J. WALTER THOMPSON COMPANY

greater even than the growth of the labor force if we are to utilize the expected increase in productivity per worker.

The basic pressure for accelerated economic growth will have an important impact on the income distribution of our families and on opportunities for a dramatic rise in living standards.

The Standard of Living in a Trillion-Dollar Economy

We must increase our total sales of goods and services to consumers by about $215 billion in the next decade to keep pace with our increasing productive ability (See Chart No. 2). This much expansion in consumer demand is basic to the economic growth challenge of supplying 20 million more non-agricultural jobs for our growing labor force in the next ten years.

If our productivity per capita increases at only the average annual 2.4 percent rate of the last 25 years, by 1975 our total production of goods and services in the United States should grow to over $1,000 billion (one trillion dollars) compared with the $670 billion level in 1965.

To support the $1,000 billion production economy, which we can and must have by 1975 to avoid general unemployment and underutilization of our productive ability, we must add the huge amount of about $215 billion in sales to consumers to raise the 1965 level of personal consumption from $425 billion to a total of $640 billion in 1975.

Chart 2
$1,000 BILLION U.S. PRODUCTION BY 1975
ADDS $215 BILLION TO CONSUMPTION
OPPORTUNITY FOR 51% HIGHER LIVING STANDARDS

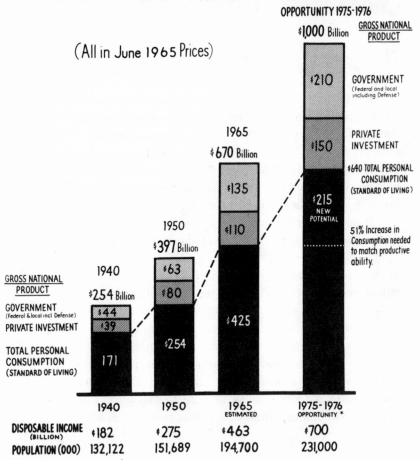

(All in June 1965 Prices)

OPPORTUNITY 1975-1976

$1000 Billion   GROSS NATIONAL PRODUCT

GOVERNMENT (Federal and local including Defense) $210

1965
$670 Billion

PRIVATE INVESTMENT $150

$640 TOTAL PERSONAL CONSUMPTION (STANDARD OF LIVING)

$135

$215 NEW POTENTIAL

1950
$397 Billion

$110

51% Increase in Consumption needed to match productive ability.

GROSS NATIONAL PRODUCT

1940
$254 Billion

$63

$80

GOVERNMENT (Federal & local incl Defense) $44

$425

PRIVATE INVESTMENT $39

$254

TOTAL PERSONAL CONSUMPTION (STANDARD OF LIVING)

171

	1940	1950	1965 ESTIMATED	1975-1976 OPPORTUNITY *
DISPOSABLE INCOME (BILLION)	$182	$275	$463	$700
POPULATION (000)	132,122	151,689	194,700	231,000

* Based on Probable Population Growth and a minimum increase in production per capita of 2.4% per year.

J. WALTER THOMPSON COMPANY

The velocity of change in living standards needed to match these conservative estimates of future productive ability nearly staggers the imagination. To add $215 billion to the U.S. standard of living means adding over the next *ten years,* in addition to the present high level of consumption, over 1¼ times as much as the entire growth in consumption in the 320 years from the landing of the Mayflower at Plymouth in 1620 to the best prewar year, 1940! Total consumption in 1940 was only $171 billion in terms of today's dollars.

That means rapid changes in markets and in the purchasing habits and consumption desires of people. And this velocity of increase in consumer demand and standard of living concepts will have to rely heavily on the educational and desire-guidance force of advertising and public relations.

Discretionary Spending Power Potential

An important factor in changing and expanding market opportunities is the rapid growth in *discretionary spending power* of our population resulting from increased productivity per capita. Discretionary spending power is defined here as the surplus spending power above what would be required to supply the same per capita standard of living for the basic necessities of food, clothing, and shelter as equivalent to the *1950* actual standard of living after taking into account present prices. The discretionary spending power just since 1950 has increased from 41 percent of total disposable income, after taxes, to 56 percent in 1965, and by 1975 its share of the greatly increased income could grow to 66 percent.

Discretionary spending power, based on a 1950 standard of living concept, grew 202 percent between 1950 and 1965 (*See* Chart No. 3 and Table No. 1). It could grow another 78 percent over 1965 to an impressive total of about $460 billion by 1975 if we reach our minimum production opportunity of $1,000 billion and succeed in keeping consumer prices reasonably near the present range with an index of about 110 (1957–59 = 100). There is a likelihood of a 35 percent growth in discretionary spending power by 1970.

This means that families moving up to better income groups, could, if they desired, take on a greater physical consumption of many products than could their prewar counterparts in similar income groups. They could upgrade substantially their health and personal care interests. The additional purchasing power is there even with higher prices, but the interest and desire has to be created.

Increased Financial Equity of Individuals

Another startling indication of the financial strength and latent purchasing power of consumers is the $494 billion addition to the net financial equity of individuals in the last seven years (*See* Chart No. 4).

At the start of 1958 total financial assets of individuals in the United States totaled $756 billion. After deducting liabilities (mortgage debt, consumer debt, and securities loans) the individuals' net equity was *$616 billion.* At the

Chart 3
DISCRETIONARY SPENDING POWER GROWTH 202% FROM 1950 TO 1965 IN U.S. OPPORTUNITY FOR 78% FURTHER GROWTH IN NEXT DECADE

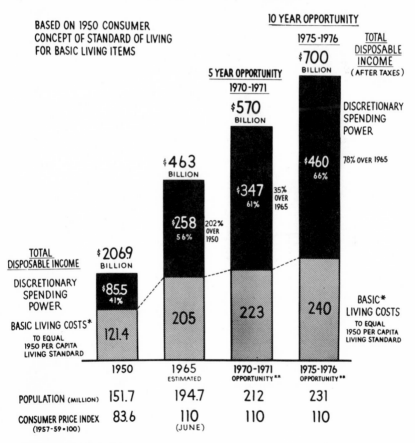

BASED ON 1950 CONSUMER
CONCEPT OF STANDARD OF LIVING
FOR BASIC LIVING ITEMS

10 YEAR OPPORTUNITY

1975-1976
$700
BILLION

TOTAL
DISPOSABLE
INCOME
(AFTER TAXES)

5 YEAR OPPORTUNITY
1970-1971

$570
BILLION

DISCRETIONARY
SPENDING
POWER

$463
BILLION

$460
66%

78% OVER 1965

$347
61%

35%
OVER
1965

$258
56%

202%
OVER
1950

TOTAL
DISPOSABLE INCOME

$206.9
BILLION

DISCRETIONARY
SPENDING
POWER

$85.5
41%

205

223

240

BASIC*
LIVING COSTS
TO EQUAL
1950 PER CAPITA
LIVING STANDARD

BASIC LIVING COSTS*
TO EQUAL
1950 PER CAPITA
LIVING STANDARD

121.4

	1950	1965 ESTIMATED	1970-1971 OPPORTUNITY**	1975-1976 OPPORTUNITY**
POPULATION (MILLION)	151.7	194.7	212	231
CONSUMER PRICE INDEX (1957-59=100)	83.6	110 (JUNE)	110	110

* Basic Living Costs of Food, Clothing, Shelter
** Based on Production Potential of $825 Billion by 1970-1971 and $1,000 Billion (One Trillion Dollars) by 1975-1976

J. WALTER THOMPSON COMPANY

Table 1

GROWTH OF DISCRETIONARY SPENDING POWER SINCE 1950

(using 1950 standard of living for food, clothing and shelter expenditures per capita as base — corrected for price changes and population growth)

Year	Total Disposable Income After Taxes	Basic Living Cost To Equal 1950 Per Capita Standard	Discretionary Spending Power	Personal Net Savings
	(Billion)	(Billion)	(Billion)	(Billion)
1950	$206.9	$121.4	$ 85.5	$31.1
1951	226.6	133.5	93.1	17.3
1952	238.3	138.6	99.7	18.2
1953	252.6	142.0	110.6	18.3
1954	257.4	145.5	111.9	16.4
1955	275.3	147.4	127.9	15.8
1956	293.2	152.0	141.2	20.6
1957	308.5	160.0	148.5	20.8
1958	318.8	167.3	151.5	22.3
1959	337.3	171.5	165.8	19.1

1960	350.0	177.8	172.2	17.0
1961	364.4	183.0	181.4	21.2
1962	385.3	187.4	197.9	21.6
1963	403.8	192.8	211.0	20.5
1964	435.8	198.0	237.8	26.3
1965 Est.	463.0	205.0	258.0	26.0
% Increase				
1950–1965	+124%	+69%	+202%	+98%
1960–1965	+32%	+15%	+50%	+53%
Opportunity*				
1970–1971	$570.0	$223.0	$347.0	$30.0
1975–1976	700.0	240.0	460.0	40.0

* Calculated on basis of total production reaching $670 billion in 1965, $825 billion by 1970–1971, and $1,000 billion (one trillion dollars) by 1975–1976, with consumer prices index at 110% of 1957–1959 average.

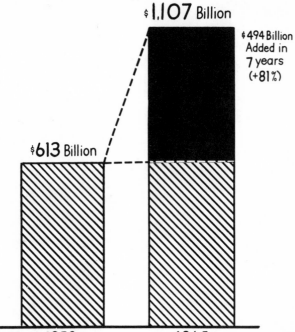

Chart 4
$494 BILLION ADDED PURCHASING POWER
IN 7 YEARS — 1958 TO 1965

INDIVIDUALS' NET FINANCIAL EQUITY

$1,107 Billion

$494 Billion
Added in
7 years
(+81%)

$613 Billion

START OF YEAR	1958		1965		INCREASE IN 7 YEARS	
Financial Assets of Individuals						
CASH & SAVINGS SHARES	$208	billion	$352	billion	$144	billion
RESERVES (INS. & PENSION)	184	"	$290	"	106	"
SECURITIES	364	"	730	"	366	"
TOTAL FINANCIAL ASSETS	$756	"	$1,372	"	$616	"
LESS LIABILITIES	143	"	265	"	122	"
NET EQUITY	$613	"	$1,107	"	$494	"

Note: Increase in net equity does not include the substantial growth of equity in homes, farms, farm machinery, automobiles and other physical assets.

J. WALTER THOMPSON COMPANY

Source: Securities and Exchange Commission

start of 1965 total financial assets were $1,372 *billion* with a new equity of $1,107 *billion* — over one trillion dollars!

The increase in net financial strength of individuals in the seven years was $494 billion, or 81 percent! This increase in net equity does not include the substantial growth of equity in homes, farms, farm machinery, automobiles, and other physical assets of individuals. Farm proprietors' net equities alone increased $31 billion in the seven years 1958 to 1965.

This magnitude of growth of net financial assets of United States individuals — about $71 billion a year — rather dwarfs the importance of the tempory $3 to $4 billion unfavorable United States balance of payments which caused such an alarm over gold. So the purchasing power available for raising the standard of living in the United States or for world investment has never been higher.

Just in the last four years — January 1, 1962 to an estimated figure for January 1, 1966 — *liquid assets* held by the public have increased $145 billion from $424.6 billion January 1, 1962 to an estimated $569.6 billion by January 1, 1966.

The Revolutionary Expansion of Family Real Income

In the fourteen years from 1950 to 1964, the number of families in the United States with *real* incomes over $10,000 increased 275 percent in terms of constant 1964 dollars (*See* Chart No. 5). In other words, by 1964 there were nearly four times as many families (of two or more

Chart 5
FAMILY REAL INCOME EXPANDING
REVOLUTIONARY CHANGE IN 14 YEARS 1950-1964

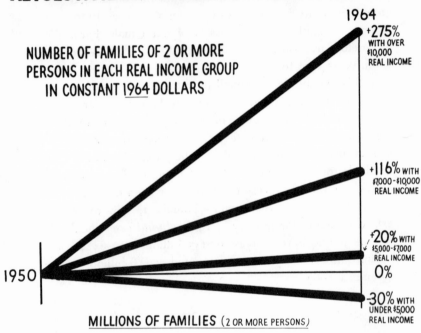

NUMBER OF FAMILIES OF 2 OR MORE
PERSONS IN EACH REAL INCOME GROUP
IN CONSTANT 1964 DOLLARS

1964

+275% WITH OVER $10,000 REAL INCOME

+116% WITH $7,000-$10,000 REAL INCOME

+20% WITH $5,000-$7,000 REAL INCOME

0%

-30% WITH UNDER $5,000 REAL INCOME

1950

MILLIONS OF FAMILIES (2 OR MORE PERSONS)

FAMILY INCOME	1950		1964	
	CURRENT DOLLARS	1964 DOLLARS	ACTUAL 1964 DOLLARS	% CHANGE
OVER $10,000	1.2	2.8	10.5	+275%
$7,000 TO $10,000	2.4	5.1	11.0	+116%
$5,000 TO $7,000	5.6	8.0	9.6	+20%
UNDER $5,000	30.7	24.0	16.7	-30%
TOTAL FAMILIES (MILLIONS)	39.9	39.9	47.8	+20%
MEDIAN INCOME	$3,319	$4,293	$6,569	+53%

Source Bureau of the Census Series P-60, No 47 - Sept 24, 1965

J. WALTER THOMPSON COMPANY

persons) with real purchasing power of over $10,000 annually than existed fourteen years before.

The number of families with a real purchasing power between $7,000 and $10,000 more than doubled (116 percent increase). Thus the number over $7,000 jumped to nearly three times the number in 1950: from 7.9 million families to 21.5 million in 1964.

The total of families with over $5,000 of real purchasing power (in terms of income in constant 1964 dollars with inflation removed) nearly doubled from 15.9 million or 40 percent of the total in 1950 to 31.1 million or 65 percent of the total in 1964; while those with under $5,000 real income dropped from 24.0 million to 16.7 million — a decline of −30 percent in numbers.

By 1975 the average personal income per household should exceed $11,300, and the number of families of two or more persons with real purchasing power of over $10,000 should grow to over 28 million, or over 2½ times the 10.8 million in 1964, and to over ten times the number in 1950.

With the possibility of the average total personal income per household in the United States reaching over $11,300 when our production level reaches one trillion dollars ten years from now, the climb upward in income groups will continue to expand the opportunities for upgrading the standard of living by consumers.

The Future Growth of Average Income

$1,000 billion of production by 1975 should provide about $790 billion of personal income for consumers — an

average of $11,300 per household for the 70 million house-
holds we are expected to have in 1975. This average income per household would be about 23 percent above the
average of $9,170 in 1965.

Table No. 2 shows how our increased productivity
could expand personal income and purchasing power
per household over the next decade.

Market Saturation Points

The 1961 studies for revision of the consumer price
index by the United States Bureau of Labor Statistics,
showing the expenditure patterns of families in different
income groups in the United States, point quite clearly
to the fallacy of thinking that we have reached a "mature"
economy, one in which consumer markets are saturated
and latent needs are satiated. Such thinking leads to re-
liance upon government spending to create jobs and attempts to regulate and curtail the private initiative or
profit incentive that can lead to greater achievement.

The study, for example, shows that in 1961 families
with above-average income spent considerably more for
food prepared at home than families with below-average
income. An even greater range was apparent for household operations (*See* Chart No. 6).

Average expenditures per family in 1961 for food
prepared at home ranged from $511 per family for the
21 percent whose incomes after taxes were below $3,000
to $1,930, nearly four times as much, for the 2.4 percent of
families with incomes over $15,000. Also, these better in-
come families spent over ten times as much on household

Table 2

INCREASED PRODUCTIVITY, PERSONAL INCOME, AND PURCHASING POWER

In Current Dollars (not corrected for inflation between 1940 and 1965)	Total Production (Billions)	Personal Income (Billions)	Households (Thousands)	Average Income Per Household (Before Taxes)
1940	$ 99.7	$ 78.3	34,949	$2,240
1950	284.8	227.6	43,554	5,225
1965 (2nd Quarter)	665.9	524.9	57,251	9,170
Opportunity (in terms of 1965 prices)				
1970–1971 (in 5 years)	$825.0	$655.0	63,800	$10,265
1975–1976 (in 10 years)	$1,000.0	$790.0	70,000	$11,300

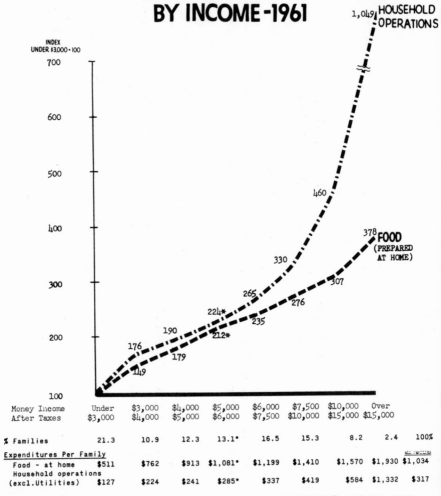

Chart 6
FOOD & HOUSEHOLD SUPPLIES MARKET
BY INCOME -1961

1,049 HOUSEHOLD OPERATIONS

INDEX
UNDER $3,000 = 100

700

600

500

400

300

200

100

460

378 FOOD
(PREPARED AT HOME)

330

307

265
276

224*
235

190
212*

176
179

149

Money Income After Taxes	Under $3,000	$3,000 $4,000	$4,000 $5,000	$5,000 $6,000	$6,000 $7,500	$7,500 $10,000	$10,000 $15,000	Over $15,000	100%
% Families	21.3	10.9	12.3	13.1*	16.5	15.3	8.2	2.4	100%
Expenditures Per Family									ALL FAMILIES
Food - at home	$511	$762	$913	$1,081*	$1,199	$1,410	$1,570	$1,930	$1,034
Household operations (excl.Utilities)	$127	$224	$241	$285*	$337	$419	$584	$1,332	$317

Based on BLS Report Number 238 - April 1964 - CONSUMER EXPENDITURES AND INCOMES 1961 - Table 1C. Based on U. S. urban families and single consumers (estimated number of families in universe 40,130,000).

*Median Average.

operations — a classification that includes household pa-
per supplies, soaps and detergents, etc., but which does
not include household utilities such as electricity or purchase of household equipment.

Even excluding the very highest level, the 2.4 percent
with incomes over $15,000, it is significant to note that
the 1961 family in the group whose income is around
$10,000, the estimated average urban family income ten
years from now, represents a food market *45 percent
greater* than the $5,000 to $6,000 median income family
of 1961 — and a household operations market that is *100
percent greater*. In addition to increased family income,
the number of households expected by 1975–1976 will be
about 25 percent greater than that of 1965. This could
indicate a potential increase at present prices of over
80 percent in the total consumer dollars expended for
food prepared at home. Likewise, the 1975 market for
household supplies could become over 2½ times as large
if families moving up in income are educated to take on
the 1961 pattern of consumption of the $10,000 family.

Charts No. 6 through No. 16 show, for different areas
of our standard of living, how markets could be expanded
and upgraded as productivity and income increases.

With a potential growth to over one trillion dollars of
production in the next decade, which could provide an
average income of $11,300 per household, many markets
could more than double without excessive luxury or ex-
ceeding the present way of life of families who are now at
the $10,000 income level.

For example, assuming a 25 percent increase in
households and a movement upward to the 1961 expendi-

ture pattern of the $10,000 income, the following rough estimates of increased potential would apply:

Table 3

POTENTIAL INCREASES IN CONSUMPTION

	Total Consumer Expenditures for:	Potential Increases
Chart 6	Food Prepared at Home	80%
Chart 6	Household Operations & Supplies	155%
Chart 7	House Furnishing	130%
Chart 8	Household Utilities	90%
Chart 9	Clothing	190%
Chart 10	Personal Care	105%
Chart 11	Medical Care	110%
Chart 12	Personal Insurance	195%
Chart 13	Gifts & Contributions (welfare-charity-religion)	210%
Chart 14	Reading	140%
Chart 15	Recreation	225%
Chart 16	Automobile Transportation	120%

Of course these potentials are not likely to be realized unless desires are stimulated so that people will upgrade their standard of living voluntarily. That is why advertising and selling can be expected to play an increasingly important role in our economy.

Growth in the Number of Households

The growth in the number of households in the United States averaged approximately 900,000 annually in the fifteen-year period 1950 to 1965 (*See* Chart No.

Chart 7
HOUSE FURNISHINGS MARKET
BY INCOME -1961

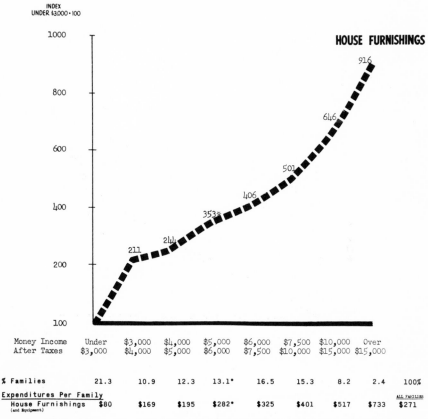

INDEX
UNDER $3,000 · 100

HOUSE FURNISHINGS

916

646

501

406

353*

244

211

Money Income After Taxes	Under $3,000	$3,000 $4,000	$4,000 $5,000	$5,000 $6,000	$6,000 $7,500	$7,500 $10,000	$10,000 $15,000	Over $15,000
% Families	21.3	10.9	12.3	13.1*	16.5	15.3	8.2	2.4	100%

Expenditures Per Family

House Furnishings (and Equipment)	$80	$169	$195	$282*	$325	$401	$517	$733	ALL FAMILIES $271

Based on BLS Report Number 238 – April 1964 – CONSUMER EXPENDITURES AND INCOMES 1961 – Table 1C. Based on U. S. urban families and single consumers (estimated number of families in universe 40,130,000).

*Median Average.

J. WALTER THOMPSON COMPANY

Chart 8
HOUSEHOLD UTILITIES MARKET
BY INCOME -1961

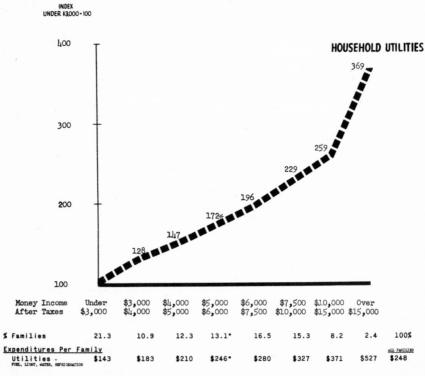

INDEX
UNDER $3,000 = 100

HOUSEHOLD UTILITIES

400

369

300

259

229

196

172½

200

147

128

100

Money Income After Taxes	Under $3,000	$3,000 $4,000	$4,000 $5,000	$5,000 $6,000	$6,000 $7,500	$7,500 $10,000	$10,000 $15,000	Over $15,000	
% Families	21.3	10.9	12.3	13.1*	16.5	15.3	8.2	2.4	100%
Expenditures Per Family									ALL FAMILIES
Utilities - FUEL, LIGHT, WATER, REFRIGERATION	$143	$183	$210	$246*	$280	$327	$371	$527	$248

Based on BLS Report Number 238 - April 1964 - CONSUMER EXPENDITURES AND INCOMES 1961 - Table 1C. Based on U. S. urban families and single consumers (estimated number of families in universe 40,130,000).

*Median Average.

Chart 9
CLOTHING MARKET
BY INCOME -1961

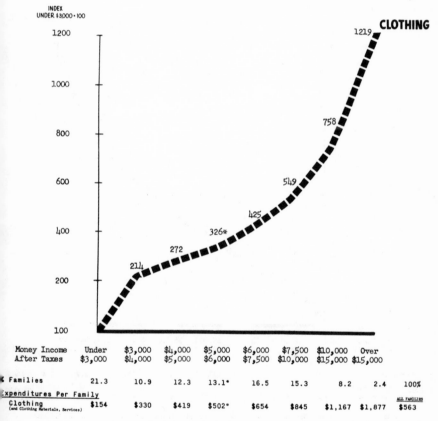

INDEX
UNDER $3,000 = 100

Money Income After Taxes	Under $3,000	$3,000 $4,000	$4,000 $5,000	$5,000 $6,000	$6,000 $7,500	$7,500 $10,000	$10,000 $15,000	Over $15,000	
% Families	21.3	10.9	12.3	13.1*	16.5	15.3	8.2	2.4	100%
Expenditures Per Family									
Clothing (and Clothing Materials, Services)	$154	$330	$419	$502*	$654	$845	$1,167	$1,877	ALL FAMILIES $563

Based on BLS Report Number 238 – April 1964 – CONSUMER EXPENDITURES AND INCOMES 1961 – Table 1C.   Based
on U. S. urban families and single consumers (estimated number of families in universe 40,130,000).

*Median Average.

Chart 10
PERSONAL CARE MARKET
BY INCOME -1961

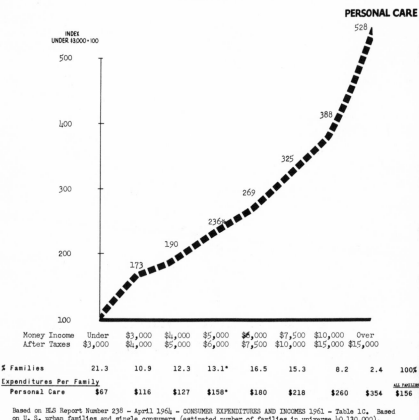

PERSONAL CARE

INDEX
UNDER $3,000 = 100

Money Income After Taxes	Under $3,000	$3,000 $4,000	$4,000 $5,000	$5,000 $6,000	$6,000 $7,500	$7,500 $10,000	$10,000 $15,000	Over $15,000	
% Families	21.3	10.9	12.3	13.1*	16.5	15.3	8.2	2.4	100%
Expenditures Per Family									ALL FAMILIES
Personal Care	$67	$116	$127	$158*	$180	$218	$260	$354	$156

Based on BLS Report Number 238 — April 1964 — CONSUMER EXPENDITURES AND INCOMES 1961 — Table 1C. Based on U. S. urban families and single consumers (estimated number of families in universe 40,130,000).

*Median Average.

Chart 11
MEDICAL CARE MARKET
BY INCOME -1961

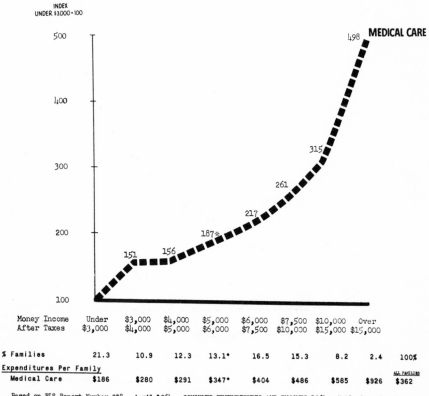

Money Income After Taxes	Under $3,000	$3,000 $4,000	$4,000 $5,000	$5,000 $6,000	$6,000 $7,500	$7,500 $10,000	$10,000 $15,000	Over $15,000	
% Families	21.3	10.9	12.3	13.1*	16.5	15.3	8.2	2.4	100%
Expenditures Per Family									ALL FAMILIES
Medical Care	$186	$280	$291	$347*	$404	$486	$585	$926	$362

Based on BLS Report Number 238 – April 1964 – CONSUMER EXPENDITURES AND INCOMES 1961 – Table 1C. Based on U. S. urban families and single consumers (estimated number of families in universe 40,130,000).

*Median Average.

J. WALTER THOMPSON COMPANY

Chart 12
PERSONAL INSURANCE MARKET
BY INCOME-1961

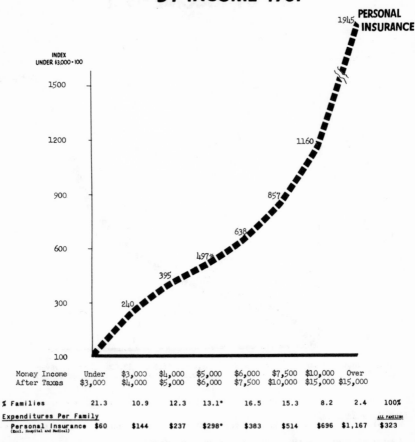

Money Income After Taxes	Under $3,000	$3,000 $4,000	$4,000 $5,000	$5,000 $6,000	$6,000 $7,500	$7,500 $10,000	$10,000 $15,000	Over $15,000	
% Families	21.3	10.9	12.3	13.1*	16.5	15.3	8.2	2.4	100%
Expenditures Per Family									ALL FAMILIES
Personal Insurance (Excl. Hospital and Medical)	$60	$144	$237	$298*	$383	$514	$696	$1,167	$323

Based on HLS Report Number 238 - April 1964 - CONSUMER EXPENDITURES AND INCOMES 1961 - Table 1C. Based on U. S. urban families and single consumers (estimated number of families in universe 40,130,000).

*Median Average.

J. WALTER THOMPSON COMPANY

Chart 13
GIFTS AND CONTRIBUTIONS
BY INCOME-1961

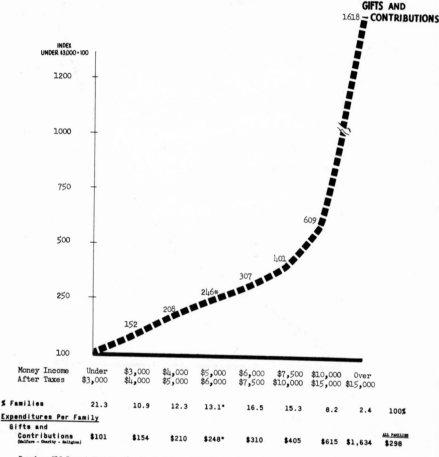

GIFTS AND
CONTRIBUTIONS

INDEX
UNDER $3,000 = 100

1200

1000

750

500

250

100

1618

609

401

307

246*

208

152

Money Income After Taxes	Under $3,000	$3,000 $4,000	$4,000 $5,000	$5,000 $6,000	$6,000 $7,500	$7,500 $10,000	$10,000 $15,000	Over $15,000	
% Families	21.3	10.9	12.3	13.1*	16.5	15.3	8.2	2.4	100%
Expenditures Per Family									
Gifts and Contributions (Welfare - Charity - Religion)	$101	$154	$210	$248*	$310	$405	$615	$1,634	ALL FAMILIES $298

Based on BLS Report Number 238 – April 1964 – CONSUMER EXPENDITURES AND INCOMES 1961 – Table 1C. Based on U. S. urban families and single consumers (estimated number of families in universe 40,130,000).

*Median Average.

Chart 14
READING EXPENDITURES
BY INCOME-1961

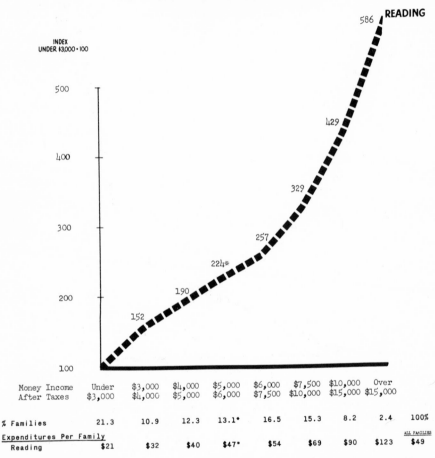

INDEX
UNDER $3,000 · 100

READING

Money Income After Taxes	Under $3,000	$3,000 $4,000	$4,000 $5,000	$5,000 $6,000	$6,000 $7,500	$7,500 $10,000	$10,000 $15,000	Over $15,000	
% Families	21.3	10.9	12.3	13.1*	16.5	15.3	8.2	2.4	100%
Expenditures Per Family Reading	$21	$32	$40	$47*	$54	$69	$90	$123	ALL FAMILIES $49

Based on BLS Report Number 238 — April 1964 — CONSUMER EXPENDITURES AND INCOMES 1961 — Table 1C. Based on U. S. urban families and single consumers (estimated number of families in universe 40,130,000).

*Median Average.

J. WALTER THOMPSON COMPANY

Chart 15
RECREATION MARKET
BY INCOME -1961

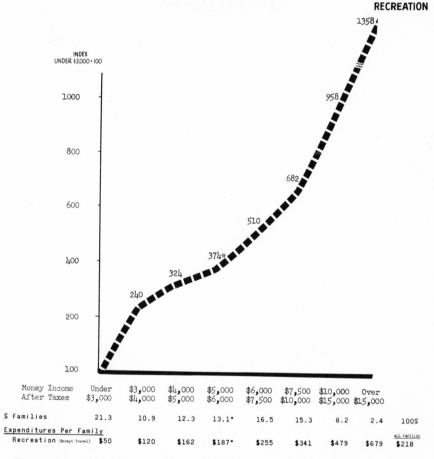

RECREATION

INDEX
UNDER $3,000 = 100

1358

1000

958

800

682

600

510

400   374*

324

240

200

100

Money Income After Taxes	Under $3,000	$3,000 $4,000	$4,000 $5,000	$5,000 $6,000	$6,000 $7,500	$7,500 $10,000	$10,000 $15,000	Over $15,000	
% Families	21.3	10.9	12.3	13.1*	16.5	15.3	8.2	2.4	100%
Expenditures Per Family Recreation (Except Travel)	$50	$120	$162	$187*	$255	$341	$479	$679	ALL FAMILIES $218

Based on BLS Report Number 238 - April 1964 - CONSUMER EXPENDITURES AND INCOMES 1961 - Table 1C. Based on U. S. urban families and single consumers (estimated number of families in universe 40,130,000).

*Median Average.

J. WALTER THOMPSON COMPANY

Chart 16
AUTOMOBILE TRANSPORTATION MARKET BY INCOME -1961

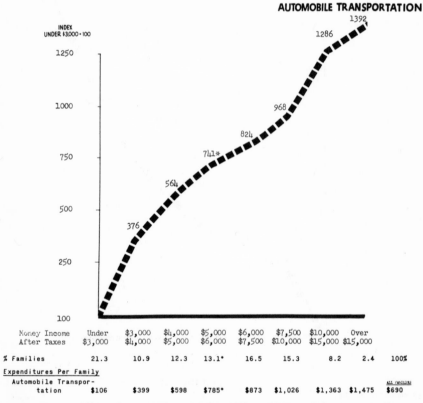

AUTOMOBILE TRANSPORTATION

Money Income After Taxes	Under $3,000	$3,000 $4,000	$4,000 $5,000	$5,000 $6,000	$6,000 $7,500	$7,500 $10,000	$10,000 $15,000	Over $15,000	
% Families	21.3	10.9	12.3	13.1*	16.5	15.3	8.2	2.4	100%
Expenditures Per Family									ALL FAMILIES
Automobile Transportation	$106	$399	$598	$785*	$873	$1,026	$1,363	$1,475	$690

Based on BLS Report Number 238 – April 1964 – CONSUMER EXPENDITURES AND INCOMES 1961 – Table 1C. Based on U. S. urban families and single consumers (estimated number of families in universe 40,130,000).

*Median Average.

J. WALTER THOMPSON COMPANY

17). The average growth from 1950 to 1955 was 864,000; from 1955 to 1960 the growth rate increased to 985,000; then, in the period 1960 to 1965, the average dropped to 890,000.

An acceleration in the formation of households became evident in the period from March 1964 to March 1965 when the number grew by 1,255,000. This was 56 percent greater than the 807,000 growth in the previous year from March 1963 to March 1964, and over double the growth of 537,000 between March 1962 and March 1963.

Recent projections for the next five years indicate an increase of about 6.6 million households — or an annual growth of more than 1.3 million. The increase of married couples with their own households for this period is expected to double the 1960 to 1965 rate.

This potential growth in households, when combined with the opportunity for upgrading the living standards as family real incomes increase, points to opportunities for substantial increases in total markets over the next decade. The increase in demand needed to provide 20 million additional non-agricultural jobs does not seem exorbitant.

The Rise in Education Level

Another rapidly changing characteristic of our population that points to opportunities for improved living standards is the level of education. By July 1964 the number of adults (over 20) with a full high-school education was 2½ times as great as in 1940 (*See* Chart No. 18).

This adult population, containing nearly 60 million

Chart 17
RAPID GROWTH IN HOUSEHOLDS PROBABLE AFTER 1965

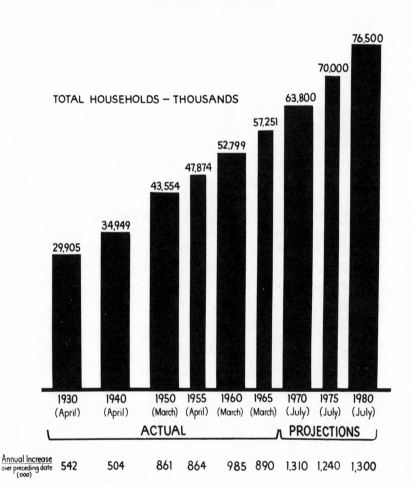

TOTAL HOUSEHOLDS — THOUSANDS

	1930 (April)	1940 (April)	1950 (March)	1955 (April)	1960 (March)	1965 (March)	1970 (July)	1975 (July)	1980 (July)
Total Households	29,905	34,949	43,554	47,874	52,799	57,251	63,800	70,000	76,500
	← ACTUAL →						← PROJECTIONS →		
Annual Increase over preceding date (000)	542	504	861	864	985	890	1,310	1,240	1,300

Bureau of the Census, P-20, No.123, April 11, 1963 & P-20, No.140, July 2, 1965

Chart 18
RAPID RISE IN EDUCATION LEVEL

156% INCREASE SINCE 1940 IN NUMBER OF HIGH SCHOOL GRADUATES IN U.S. ADULT POPULATION
38% ADDITIONAL INCREASE BY 1974

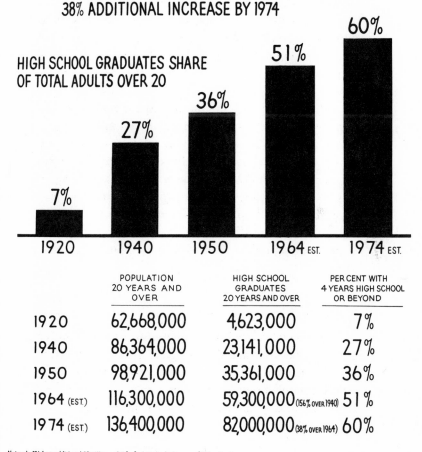

HIGH SCHOOL GRADUATES SHARE
OF TOTAL ADULTS OVER 20

	7%	27%	36%	51%	60%
	1920	1940	1950	1964 EST.	1974 EST.

	POPULATION 20 YEARS AND OVER	HIGH SCHOOL GRADUATES 20 YEARS AND OVER	PER CENT WITH 4 YEARS HIGH SCHOOL OR BEYOND
1920	62,668,000	4,623,000	7%
1940	86,364,000	23,141,000	27%
1950	98,921,000	35,361,000	36%
1964 (EST.)	116,300,000	59,300,000 (156% OVER 1940)	51%
1974 (EST.)	136,400,000	82,000,000 (38% OVER 1964)	60%

Note – In 1964 an additional 23 million or 20% of adults had 1-3 years of high school.

high school graduates in 1964, contrasts with an adult population of 23 million graduates in 1940 or a population of about 4½ million graduates shortly after World War I, in 1920.

This means that today we have quite a different population in terms of education than we had in the prewar period, and that this change can have a significant influence on living and reading habits and therefore on the "social mobility" of the population. It can offer favorable opportunities for expansion of consumption of items that fit into an upgraded standard of living in quality, comfort, convenience, variety, cultural tastes, and health interests.

The rapid change in educational composition of our population will continue. By 1974 the estimated 82 million high-school graduates in our adult population will represent about 60 percent of the total number of persons 20 years and over. That is a numerical increase of 38 percent over 1964, while the adult population will grow only 18 percent. Total college graduates increased from 3.9 million in 1940 to 8.1 million in 1960, and by 1974 there should be 12.5 million — or over three times the number in 1940.

Education and Income

The 1963 Census Bureau analysis of the relationship between education and the income of males over fourteen revealed that education is an important factor in America's increased productive ability, since, in general, income received is an index of one's contribution to total production. On the average, the median income in 1963 increased with each increase in level of education.

Those with four years of high school enjoyed incomes 150 percent higher than those with less than eight years of elementary school; and those who had received four or more years of college training had incomes averaging 98 percent above those with only one to three years of high school.

With the growing numbers of our population joining the ranks of high-school and college graduates, we should anticipate even more rapid improvement in productive ability, income, standard of living, and social concepts and goals.

There are startling differences in the level of school enrollment in the United States and leading European countries in the age groups of high-school and college material as shown in Table No. 4.

School and College Enrollment

Total school enrollment is expected to increase 33 percent by 1975 with the most rapid growth represented by a 100 percent increase in college enrollment. Elementary school enrollment will increase 26 percent and high school enrollment, 29 percent (*See* Chart No. 19).

This rapid change in educational composition of our population along with greater discretionary income is changing the pattern of living in the United States.

The United States has definitely entered a consumption-oriented economy where more and more emphasis is being directed towards improving living standards. Even

Table 4

SCHOOL ENROLLMENT HERE AND ABROAD

	Per Cent of Each Age Group Enrolled In Full-Time School	
	15–19 years	20–24 years
United States (1963)	*75%*	*17%*
Western Europe (Late 1950's)*		
Austria	13.1%	3.7%
Belgium	31.5	5.5
Denmark	18.5	5.6
France	30.8	3.8
Germany (F.R.)	17.6	4.6
Greece	16.9	3.3
Italy	15.7	3.9
Netherlands	32.8	4.7
Norway	35.7	9.5
Portugal	8.8	3.1
Spain	13.3	3.3
Sweden	32.3	11.0
Switzerland	22.9	3.4
United Kingdom	16.8	2.4

* Twentieth Century Fund Survey — The New Europe & Its Economic Future, 1964.

though the present standards in the United States are high relative to many other areas of the world, there is increasing recognition that they could be vastly but realistically upgraded for the mass of the population and that, thus activated, latent demand can stimulate the profitable expansion of production.

Chart 19
HOW SCHOOL ENROLLMENT MAY GROW BY 1975

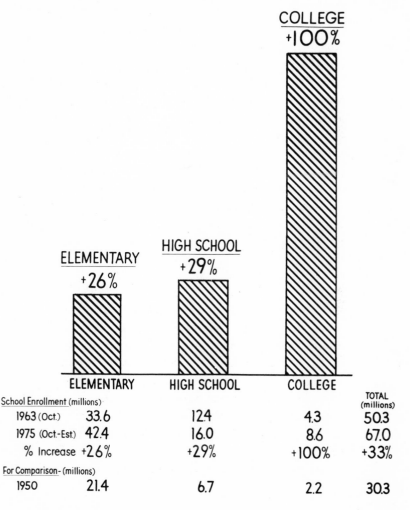

	ELEMENTARY	HIGH SCHOOL	COLLEGE	TOTAL (millions)
School Enrollment (millions)				
1963 (Oct.)	33.6	12.4	4.3	50.3
1975 (Oct.-Est.)	42.4	16.0	8.6	67.0
% Increase	+26%	+29%	+100%	+33%
For Comparison- (millions)				
1950	21.4	6.7	2.2	30.3

Source: Bureau of the Census P-25, No.232, June 22,1961 and P-20, No.129 JULY 24,1964

J. WALTER THOMPSON COMPANY

Growth in Health Interest

A change toward better family living and greater interest in health is reflected in the trend of consumer expenditures in the United States since 1947 (See Chart No. 20). Total personal consumption expenditures increased 127 percent between 1947 and 1963, but those items having to do with family living, health, and personal care have gone up considerably more than the average.

Drug-store prescription sales, for example, grew to over five times the 1947 level. Hospital expenditures, life insurance, medical and hospitalization insurance grew rapidly. Expenditures for dental care, physicians, personal care, and toilet articles and preparations all increased more than the total standard of living as measured by personal consumption expenditures.

Changing Pattern of Living in the United States

There is a trend toward increased home and family life in America that points to pressures for substantial improvement in living standards (See Chart No. 21).

This trend to home-oriented family life is reflected in the rapid increase in number of families; in a higher percentage of marriages in general and especially those at an earlier age; in an extraordinary increase in the number of children under ten in our population and, as a result, in each family, and a higher percentage of families having children; in a rapid increase in home ownership,

Chart 20
HEALTH AND PERSONAL CARE
POSTWAR TREND IN PERSONAL CONSUMPTION EXPENDITURES
1947-1963

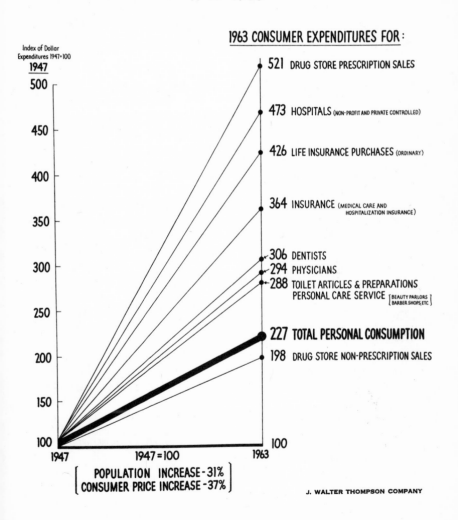

1963 CONSUMER EXPENDITURES FOR:

Index of Dollar
Expenditures 1947=100

1947

521 DRUG STORE PRESCRIPTION SALES

473 HOSPITALS (NON-PROFIT AND PRIVATE CONTROLLED)

426 LIFE INSURANCE PURCHASES (ORDINARY)

364 INSURANCE (MEDICAL CARE AND HOSPITALIZATION INSURANCE)

306 DENTISTS
294 PHYSICIANS
288 TOILET ARTICLES & PREPARATIONS
PERSONAL CARE SERVICE [BEAUTY PARLORS BARBER SHOPS, ETC]

227 TOTAL PERSONAL CONSUMPTION

198 DRUG STORE NON-PRESCRIPTION SALES

1947   1947 = 100   1963   100

[POPULATION INCREASE - 31%
CONSUMER PRICE INCREASE - 37%]

Chart 21
CHANGES IN CONSUMER EXPENDITURES SINCE 1947
REFLECT CHANGING HOME LIFE

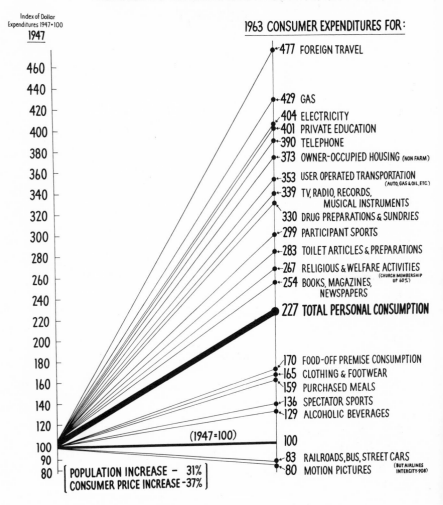

Index of Dollar
Expenditures 1947=100

1947

1963 CONSUMER EXPENDITURES FOR:

460 —
440 —
420 —
400 —
380 —
360 —
340 —
320 —
300 —
280 —
260 —
240 —
220 —
200 —
180 —
160 —
140 —
120 —
100 —
90 —
80 —

477 FOREIGN TRAVEL

429 GAS
404 ELECTRICITY
401 PRIVATE EDUCATION
390 TELEPHONE
373 OWNER-OCCUPIED HOUSING (NON FARM)
353 USER OPERATED TRANSPORTATION (AUTO, GAS & OIL, ETC.)
339 TV, RADIO, RECORDS, MUSICAL INSTRUMENTS
330 DRUG PREPARATIONS & SUNDRIES
299 PARTICIPANT SPORTS
283 TOILET ARTICLES & PREPARATIONS
267 RELIGIOUS & WELFARE ACTIVITIES (CHURCH MEMBERSHIP UP 60%)
254 BOOKS, MAGAZINES, NEWSPAPERS
227 TOTAL PERSONAL CONSUMPTION
170 FOOD-OFF PREMISE CONSUMPTION
165 CLOTHING & FOOTWEAR
159 PURCHASED MEALS
136 SPECTATOR SPORTS
129 ALCOHOLIC BEVERAGES

(1947=100)   100

83 RAILROADS, BUS, STREET CARS
80 MOTION PICTURES (BUT AIRLINES INTERCITY-908)

[POPULATION INCREASE – 31%]
[CONSUMER PRICE INCREASE -37%]

Source: Office of Business Economics U.S. Dept of Commerce - July 1964

J. WALTER THOMPSON COMPANY

and in expenditures for activities of home life; in a movement of population to the suburbs; in the rapid growth of shopping centers and self-service distribution; and in a resurgence of religious worship and church membership as shown by the growth of 60 percent in church membership from 1947 to 1963 while population was increasing only 31 percent. Church membership has been growing *twice* as fast as population! In the same period consumer expenditures for religious and welfare activities jumped 167 percent.

The change toward family living, even since 1947, is reflected in the trend of consumer expenditures. Those items having to do with the home and family living and health of the family members increased between 1947 and 1963 considerably more than the 127 percent average. Whereas expenditures for an item like spectator amusements increased only 36 percent, expenditures for participant sports increased five times as fast — or by 199 percent. Expenditures for drug preparations and sundries increased 230 percent and for reading material, 154 percent.

"The Baby Boom"

The "baby boom" since 1940 in the United States has been of such proportions that it will have a pronounced effect on market potentials and population characteristics over the next ten to fifteen years (*See* Chart No. 22).

The number of births in the United States has continued at a level far above earlier predictions by population experts. While total births have declined somewhat

Chart 22
THE BABY BOOM - SINCE 1940

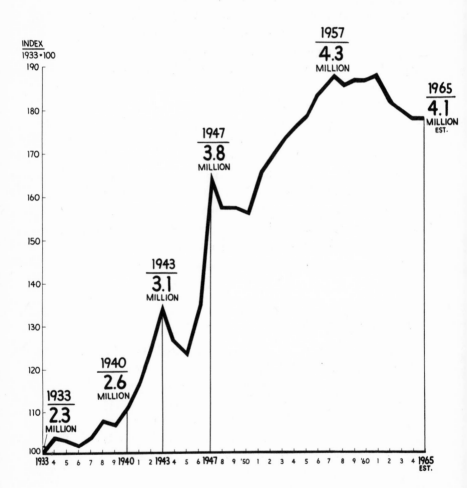

INDEX
1933 = 100

1957
4.3
MILLION

1965
4.1
MILLION
EST.

1947
3.8
MILLION

1943
3.1
MILLION

1940
2.6
MILLION

1933
2.3
MILLION

190

180

170

160

150

140

130

120

110

100

1933 4 5 6 7 8 9 1940 1 2 1943 4 5 6 1947 8 9 '50 1 2 3 4 5 6 7 8 9 '60 1 2 3 4 1965
EST.

in the last three years they have held at over four million annually for the last ten years compared with about 2½ million in 1940. This is changing the composition of families and the age distribution of the United States population.

Add 25 years to the dates shown in Chart No. 22 and it is easy to follow the rapid increase to be expected from 1965 on in the number of young people reaching the high consumption, family-formation age.

By 1975 the number of births annually is expected to reach a level of from 5 to 5½ million.

Age Distribution in the Population

As of July 1965 it was estimated that there were 90 percent more children under 10 years of age in our population than in 1940 (*See* Chart No. 23 and Table No. 5).

Table 5

CHANGES IN AGE DISTRIBUTION

Age Group	Past 25 Years 1940–1965 Percent Change	Next 10 Years 1965–1975 Percent Change
Under 10	+90%	+23%
10–19	+49	+16
20–34	+9	+40
35–49	+35	−5
50–64	+54	+15
65 and over	+103	+17
Total	+48%	+18%

Chart 23
CHANGING U.S. AGE PATTERN

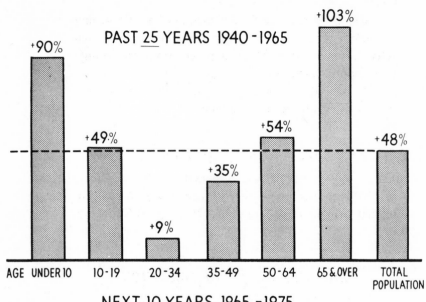

PAST 25 YEARS 1940-1965

+90% +49% +9% +35% +54% +103% +48%

AGE UNDER 10   10-19   20-34   35-49   50-64   65 & OVER   TOTAL POPULATION

NEXT 10 YEARS 1965-1975

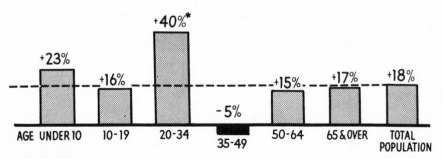

+23% +16% +40%* -5% +15% +17% +18%

AGE UNDER 10   10-19   20-34   35-49   50-64   65 & OVER   TOTAL POPULATION

* 20-24 +40%
  25-29 +53%
  30-34 +26%

This huge increase in the number of children is affecting housing requirements, food consumption, health needs, and many phases of family living. During the next few years, unusually large numbers of children will grow into the adolescent age groups where food consumption is high and where interest in many products starts.

The 25-year period from 1940 to 1965 was characterized by a rapid increase in population in the two age groups at either extreme — youngsters under 10 and persons over 65. There was an increase of only 9 percent in the number of young adults in the prime family-formation age group of 20–34.

The *next decade will be different* (*See* Chart No. 23 and Table No. 5). It will be characterized by a rapid increase in the family-formation age group, 20 to 34, and adolescents, 10 to 19, and a −5 percent decline in the middle executive group, 35–49.

Details of the rapid change in age distribution between 1940, 1950, and 1965, with projections to 1975, are shown in Table No. 6.

Families with Two or More Children

For many years American families decreased in size. Now there are pronounced indications that this trend is reversing (*See* Chart No. 24). In the twelve years between 1951 and 1963 the number of families with two or more of their own children at home increased 52 percent while total families increased only 18 percent. Thus families with two or more children have increased three times as fast as the total growth in families.

Table 6

CHANGING U.S. AGE PATTERN – 1940–1975

Distribution of U.S. Population By Age (Millions)

					Est.	Est.	% Increase	
	1940	1950	1960	Est. 1965	Est. 1975		1940 1965	1965 1975
Under 5*	11.4	17.1	20.9	21.7	27.9		90%	29%
5–9	10.7	13.3	18.8	20.4	24.0		91%	18%
Total under 10	22.1	30.4	39.7	42.1	51.9		90%	23%
10–14	11.8	11.1	16.9	18.9	21.3		60%	13%
15–19	12.3	10.7	13.5	17.0	20.5		38%	21%
Total 10–19	24.1	21.8	30.4	35.9	41.8		49%	16%
20–24	11.6	11.6	11.1	13.6	19.1		17%	40%
25–29	11.1	12.3	10.9	11.3	17.3		2%	53%
30–34	10.2	11.6	12.0	11.0	13.9		8%	26%
Total 20–34	32.9	35.5	34.0	35.9	50.3		9%	40%

35–39	9.6	11.3	12.5	12.0	11.4	25%	−5%
40–44	8.8	10.3	11.7	12.5	11.0	42%	−12%
45–49	8.2	9.1	10.9	11.5	11.7	40%	2%
Total 35–49	26.6	30.7	35.1	36.0	34.1	35%	−5%
50–54	7.2	8.3	9.7	10.6	11.9	47%	12%
55–59	5.9	7.3	8.5	9.2	10.6	56%	15%
60–64	4.8	6.1	7.1	7.8	9.3	63%	19%
Total 50–64	17.9	21.7	25.3	27.6	31.8	54%	15%
65–69	3.7	5.0	6.3	6.3	7.5	70%	19%
70–74	2.6	3.4	4.8	5.2	5.7	100%	10%
75 and over	2.6	3.9	5.6	6.6	7.9	154%	20%
Total 65 & over	8.9	12.3	16.7	18.1	21.1	103%	17%
GRAND TOTAL*	132.5	152.4	181.2	195.6	231.0	48%	18%

* Adjusted for Census under-enumeration of children under 5 years.
Figures relate to July 1. Population includes Armed Forces abroad, and Alaska and Hawaii from 1960. P-25 No. 279 — February 4, 1964.

Chart 24

IN 12 YEARS
52% INCREASE IN FAMILIES WITH TWO OR MORE CHILDREN

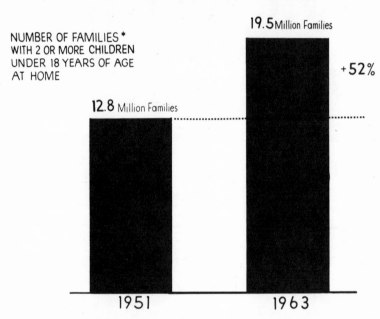

19.5 Million Families

NUMBER OF FAMILIES *
WITH 2 OR MORE CHILDREN
UNDER 18 YEARS OF AGE
AT HOME

+52%

12.8 Million Families

| 1951 | 1963 |

Total Families* **39.9 MILLION**   **47.0 MILLION** +18%

NOW 61% OF ALL FAMILIES HAVE RELATED CHILDREN

	1 CHILD	2 CHILDREN	3 OR MORE	NO RELATED CHILDREN UNDER 18
TOTAL FAMILIES* 47.0 Million 1963	19% 9.0 Million	19% 8.7 Million	23% 10.8 Million	39% 18.5 Million

* Families of two or more related persons

Now some 61 percent of all families of two or more related persons have related children under 18 in the home. This is an important factor influencing the family's market for medical care, for food, for household appliances and housing services, and for many other items. In particular, it is putting increased pressure on housing, since many of the homes in existence have only one bath or too few bedrooms. And it greatly increases the family need for hospital and medical protection and its interest in family health and diet.

Women and Skilled Workers in the Labor Force

The number of women in the labor force grew four times as rapidly in the twenty-two years between 1940 and 1962 as did the number of men (77 percent increase and 19 percent increase respectively. *See* Chart No. 25). And the major part of this increase of women workers has been among married women with families.

Between 1940 and 1962, for example, the number of married women workers jumped to a level nearly three times its size; and 54 percent of these married women workers have children at home.

This trend has been even more evident in the last few years. Between 1947 and 1962 the number of men workers in the United States increased only 12 percent while the total number of women workers increased 45 percent; and the number of married women workers jumped 97 percent! About 56 percent of our total growth in the labor force during this time has been accounted for by the addition of married women workers.

Chart 25
196% INCREASE IN MARRIED WOMEN WORKERS
SINCE 1940

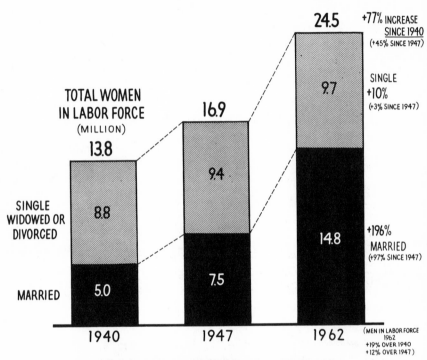

TOTAL WOMEN IN LABOR FORCE (MILLION)

24.5 +77% INCREASE SINCE 1940 (+45% SINCE 1947)

9.7 SINGLE +10% (+3% SINCE 1947)

16.9

9.4

13.8

SINGLE WIDOWED OR DIVORCED

8.8

14.8 +196% MARRIED (+97% SINCE 1947)

7.5

MARRIED 5.0

1940   1947   1962 (MEN IN LABOR FORCE 1962 +19% OVER 1940 +12% OVER 1947)

54% OF MARRIED WOMEN IN THE LABOR FORCE HAVE CHILDREN AT HOME − 1962

CHILDREN UNDER 6	CHILDREN 6 TO 17 ONLY	NO CHILDREN UNDER 18
21% 2.9 Million	33% 4.4 Million	46% 6.2 Million

Total Married Women (with Husband Present) in Labor Force 13.5 Million = 100%

Source: Manpower Report of the President - March 1963.

J. WALTER THOMPSON COMPANY

That there have been other changes in the labor force is indicated by employment practices in industry from 1940 to 1960. With a total increase in average employment of 31 percent there was a drop of −24 percent during this period in the number of unskilled workers and a drop of −52 percent in farmers and farm workers. In contrast there was an increase of 100 percent in professional and technical employment and an increase of 81 percent in clerical and sales workers. Projections for the next ten years show an acceleration of this trend toward more highly skilled occupations.

The Mobility of Our Population

The rapidity with which our markets can change is reflected by the mobility of our population (*See* Chart No. 26).

Within any five-year period the equivalent of our entire civilian population over the age of one year changes its place of residence. In the year March 1963 to March 1964, for example, the number moving totaled over 37 million, 20 percent of the 185 million civilian population one year or older. The greatest mobility was among young adults 20 to 24 years old; of these 45 percent moved their place of residence within the year. The broader group, ranging in age from 18 to 34, also moved more than the average.

New homemakers, young married females, were far above the average in changing place of residence. Fifty-seven percent of these housewives under 25, and 26 percent of the ones between 25 and 34, moved during the

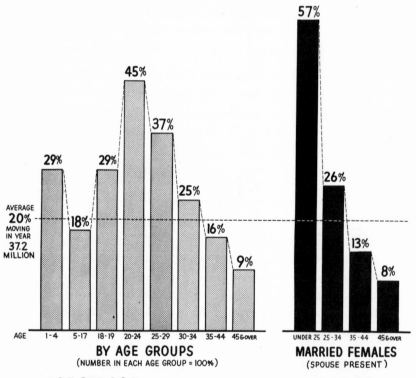

Chart 26
MOBILITY OF OUR POPULATION
PER CENT MOVING TO DIFFERENT HOUSE, MARCH 1963-MARCH 1964

TOTAL CIVILIAN POPULATION
(1 YEAR OLD OR OVER)

MARRIED FEMALES

AVERAGE
20%
MOVING
IN YEAR
37.2
MILLION

29%   18%   29%   45%   37%   25%   16%   9%

AGE   1-4   5-17   18-19   20-24   25-29   30-34   35-44   45&OVER

BY AGE GROUPS
(NUMBER IN EACH AGE GROUP = 100%)

57%   26%   13%   8%

UNDER 25   25-34   35-44   45&OVER

MARRIED FEMALES
(SPOUSE PRESENT)

TOTAL 185,312,000

TOTAL 42,045,000

100% 9.0% 26.2% 2.8% 6.6% 5.9% 6.0% 13.2% 30.3%   100% 11.3% 22.6% 24.7% 41.4%

Source: Bureau of the Census - Series P-20 No. 141 Sept. 7, 1965

year. Young-marrieds under 35 years of age represented about 34 percent of all married females in 1964. With the large increase to be expected soon in the number of young homemakers, this mobility will become an increasingly important marketing factor.

With a population shifting as rapidly as this, the importance of advertised brands, quickly identified by their packaging or symbols, is obvious. The newcomers' ability to find the familiar and preferred brand at once in the new self-service drug store, supermarket, or shopping center outlet is essential to an efficient process of distribution.

Population Shift: to the Suburbs and Off the Farm

Between 1950 and 1960 population in the suburban portion of 199 metropolitan areas grew 61 percent, while that in the central cities grew only 1 percent and in the rest of the United States, outside of the 199 Metropolitan Areas, it increased 7 percent (*See* Chart No. 27). The farm population declined 20 percent. 83 percent of the total United States growth in population between 1950 and 1960 was in the suburban sections of Metropolitan Areas outside the corporate limits of central cities as defined in 1950.

With the shift from rural areas and from many central cities to the suburban and interurban areas, over 50 percent of the counties in the United States had a drop in population in the last ten years. This rapid shift in population reflects changing living standards, changing

Chart 27

POPULATION SHIFT TO SUBURBS
REFLECTS CHANGING LIVING STANDARDS

Suburbs growing 15 times as fast as population outside of Metropolitan Areas

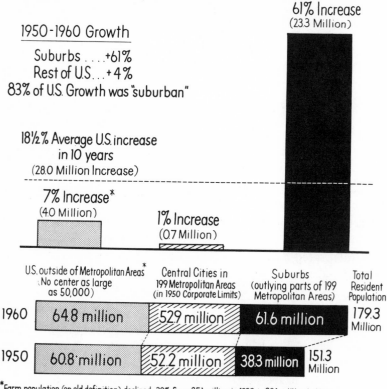

61% Increase
(23.3 Million)

1950-1960 Growth

Suburbs ....+61%
Rest of U.S....+4%
83% of U.S. Growth was "suburban"

18½% Average U.S. increase
in 10 years
(28.0 Million Increase)

7% Increase*
(4.0 Million)

1% Increase
(0.7 Million)

	U.S. outside of Metropolitan Areas* (No center as large as 50,000)	Central Cities in 199 Metropolitan Areas (in 1950 Corporate Limits)	Suburbs (outlying parts of 199 Metropolitan Areas)	Total Resident Population
1960	64.8 million	52.9 million	61.6 million	179.3 Million
1950	60.8 million	52.2 million	38.3 million	151.3 Million

*Farm population (on old definition) declined -20% from 25.1 million in 1950 to 20.1 million in 1960.
On new definition, 1960 rural farm population in April 1960 totaled only 15.7 million.

Note: 1960 Census shows, central cities population total at 57.8 million, but 4.9 million of this was in areas annexed between 1950 and 1960 classed as outside Central city in 1950. Correction has been made to show true growth of suburbs.

J. WALTER THOMPSON COMPANY

shopping habits, and the increasing trend toward family living. Between 1960 and 1963 the shift to the suburbs continued at a rate three times faster than central city growth. (Suburbs up 8.8 percent, central cities up 2.8 percent, smaller communities and rural areas up 2.7 percent versus the total United States, up 4.6 percent).

A significant feature of this shift to the suburbs is the changed composition of the population in central cities. The rapid movement of marginal income rural groups into urban industrial and non-farm jobs has resulted in higher income for this population and greatly improved consumption capacity. This trend has been particularly significant in the rapid growth of the non-white population in central cities.

In forty central cities of the Northeastern and Middle Atlantic states the non-white population *increased 50 percent* between 1950 and 1960 to an average of 22 percent of the total population. In the same period the white population *decreased −10 percent.*

Examples of this major shift of non-white population to central cities are shown in Table No. 7.

Major Regional Shifts in Population

Major regional shifts in the United States population which became so evident between 1950 and 1960 have continued to 1965 and are expected to continue in the next decade (*See* Table No. 8). The West and South may continue to grow most rapidly. As illustrated in Table No. 9, fifteen states, in particular, have shown rapid growth although their rank in percentage growth has fluctuated.

Table 7

SHIFT OF NON-WHITE POPULATION TO CENTRAL CITIES IN NORTHEAST

	% Increase in Non-White Population 1950–1960	% Decrease in White Population 1950–1960	Non-White Share of Total Central City Population 1950
Total 40 Central Cities in 32 Contiguous Standard Metropolitan Statistical Areas In Northeastern United States	+50% increase	−10% decrease	22% share
New Haven	131	−16	15
Bridgeport	127	−7	10
Hartford	97	−17	16
Newark	84	−27	34
Trenton	78	−22	23
Jersey City	78	−14	14
Boston	60	−17	10
Harrisburg	51	−19	19
Washington	47	−33	55
New York City	47	−7	15
Wilmington	45	−24	26
Baltimore	45	−16	35
Philadelphia	41	−13	27
Atlantic City	27	−15	37

SOURCE: U.S. Department of Commerce CB 61-100, August 13, 1961

Table 8

SHIFTS IN POPULATION

	1950 to 1960*	1960 to 1965**	Projected 1965 to 1975***
Total United States	18½%	8%	18½%
Northeast	13%	6%	12%
North Central	16%	5%	11%
South	17%	9%	18%
West	39%	15%	27%

Table 9

FIFTEEN FASTEST GROWING STATES

1950 to 1960*		1960 to 1965**		Projected 1965 to 1975***	
1. Florida	79%	Nevada	54%	Arizona	42%
2. Nevada	78	Arizona	24	Florida	41
3. Alaska	76	California	18	California	33
4. Arizona	74	Florida	17	Alaska	32
5. California	47	Maryland	14	New Mexico	32
6. Delaware	40	Delaware	13	Utah	27
7. Mew Mexico	40	Virginia	12	Colorado	25
8. Colorado	32	Hawaii	12	Delaware	23
9. Maryland	32	Colorado	12	Maryland	23
10. Utah	29	Alaska	12	Virginia	20
11. Hawaii	27	Connecticut	12	New Jersey	20
12. Connecticut	26	New Jersey	12	Connecticut	18
13. New Jersey	26	Utah	11	Texas	18
14. Texas	24	Texas	10	Nevada	16
15. Virginia	20	New Mexico	8	Hawaii	16

* P-25, No. 304 — April 8, 1965 — Bureau of The Census
** P-25, No. 317 — August 27, 1965 — Bureau of The Census
*** P-25, No. 301 — February 26, 1965 — Bureau of The Census

The Revolution in Distribution

Along with the climb in incomes, the shift to the suburbs, and the growth of shopping centers since 1950, there has been a revolutionary change in distribution to match the changing population. Rapid growth of discount merchandising and of self-service in supermarkets, drug stores, and other outlets is increasing the importance of advertised products with well-developed consumer preference. As an example of the revolution in distribution consider the changes in grocery-store distribution in the ten years from 1951 to 1961 (*See* Chart No. 28).

Thirty thousand supermarkets in 1961, with total sales of $38.2 billion, had an $8 billion greater total volume of business than all the 394,000 grocery stores in existence in 1951, just ten years earlier.

Representing only 12 percent of the stores in 1961, the supermarkets had 70 percent of the volume of sales. An additional group of 55,000 superettes, representing 22 percent of the stores, accounted for 22 percent of the volume. This means that self-service supermarkets and superettes, representing about one-third of the stores in the country, handled 92 percent of the grocery volume. It is no wonder that the total number of grocery stores dropped from 394,000 in 1951 to 249,000 in 1961.

Opportunity for Economic Growth and Improved Living in Western Europe

Because of potential changes in the standard of living of the population of Western Europe in the next ten

Chart 28
REVOLUTION IN GROCERY STORE DISTRIBUTION IN 10 YEARS – 1951-1961

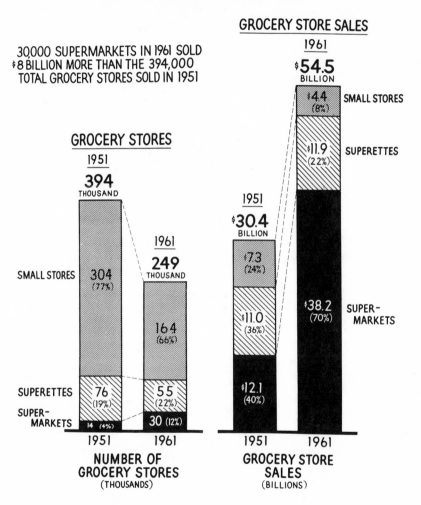

30,000 SUPERMARKETS IN 1961 SOLD $8 BILLION MORE THAN THE 394,000 TOTAL GROCERY STORES SOLD IN 1951

GROCERY STORE SALES
1961
$54.5 BILLION

$4.4 (8%) SMALL STORES

$11.9 (22%) SUPERETTES

GROCERY STORES
1951
394 THOUSAND

1951
$30.4 BILLION

SMALL STORES

304 (77%)

1961
249 THOUSAND

$7.3 (24%)

164 (66%)

$11.0 (36%)

$38.2 (70%) SUPER-MARKETS

SUPERETTES
76 (19%)
55 (22%)

SUPER-MARKETS
14 (4%)
30 (12%)

$12.1 (40%)

1951   1961
NUMBER OF GROCERY STORES
(THOUSANDS)

1951   1961
GROCERY STORE SALES
(BILLIONS)

Source: PROGRESSIVE GROCER

J. WALTER THOMPSON COMPANY

years, the western European total market for consumer goods and services should grow to over $455 billion compared with a level of about $275 billion in 1965 (*See* Chart No. 29). That is an expansion of $180 billion, 65 percent, by 1975–1976. This opportunity for growth in standard of living in Western Europe is in line with conservative estimates of growth in productive ability and purchasing power.

Adding together the minimum production opportunities of seventeen European members of the Organization for Economic Cooperation and Development (excluding Spain) we find a potential total productive ability, by 1975–1976, of over $700 billion for the anticipated population of 350 million. This is compared with $200 billion production (in terms of 1965 prices) for 274 million people in 1950.

In 1938 personal consumption in the area now constituting these seventeen European OECD countries totaled only $124 billion in terms of constant United States dollars (in June 1965 prices). Between 1938 and 1965 personal consumption grew to the $275 billion level, an addition of $151 billion in the *27 years* which included the vigorous postwar reconstruction period. And now the opportunity is for an increase of $180 billion during the next *ten years* alone!

This potential rate of growth in standard of living in Western Europe will mean rapid changes in markets and in purchasing habits and consumption desires of the people there. These changes could have an even more significant impact on world trade. The standard of living in Western Europe is expected to improve even more

Chart 29
WESTERN EUROPE (O.E.C.D. MEMBERS)
65% INCREASE IN STANDARD OF LIVING
POSSIBLE BY 1975-76

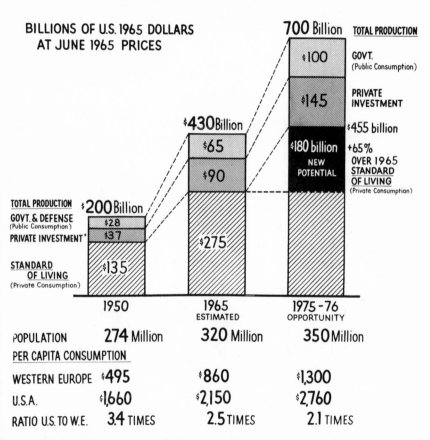

BILLIONS OF U.S. 1965 DOLLARS
AT JUNE 1965 PRICES

700 Billion — TOTAL PRODUCTION

$100 — GOVT. (Public Consumption)

$145 — PRIVATE INVESTMENT

$180 billion NEW POTENTIAL — $455 billion +65% OVER 1965 STANDARD OF LIVING (Private Consumption)

$430 Billion

$65

$90

TOTAL PRODUCTION
GOVT. & DEFENSE (Public Consumption)
PRIVATE INVESTMENT*

STANDARD OF LIVING (Private Consumption)

$200 Billion

$28

$37

$135

$275

	1950	1965 ESTIMATED	1975-76 OPPORTUNITY
POPULATION	274 Million	320 Million	350 Million
PER CAPITA CONSUMPTION			
WESTERN EUROPE	$495	$860	$1,300
U.S.A.	$1,660	$2,150	$2,760
RATIO U.S. TO W.E.	3.4 TIMES	2.5 TIMES	2.1 TIMES

Covers 17 countries – O.E.C.D. members excluding Spain.

*Construction (Residential and other) machinery and equipment, inventory change, net exports.

J. WALTER THOMPSON COMPANY

rapidly than in the United States albeit from a lower base as indicated by the level ᴗof per capita consumption.

Increase in Foreign Travel

The probable rapid rise in discretionary spending power and standard of living by 1975 in both the United States and other areas of the free world could result in a burgeoning expansion of travel and communication worldwide.

Already televised communication (via Comsat) has been proved practical for both commercial and educational use.

The impact of our rising standard of living on travel is illustrated by the trend between 1950 and 1964 when overseas travel expenditures by Americans grew 269 percent, or 2½ times as fast at the total increase of 105 percent in personal consumption expenditures (*See* Chart No. 30). And the number of travelers increased 228 percent, or 3¾ times the total standard of living increase of 61 percent in constant dollars. The more developed countries of Western Europe and Japan had the greatest increases in travel.

A projection of these travel trends to the trillion-dollar economy possible by 1975 is illustrated in Chart No. 31. Indications are that there is a potential for three-fold growth in the expenditures for foreign travel by Americans reaching a total of about $11 billion at the end of the next decade.

Chart 30

OVERSEAS TRAVEL EXPENDITURES IN LAST 14 YEARS GREW OVER 2½ TIMES AS FAST AS STANDARD OF LIVING IN U.S.

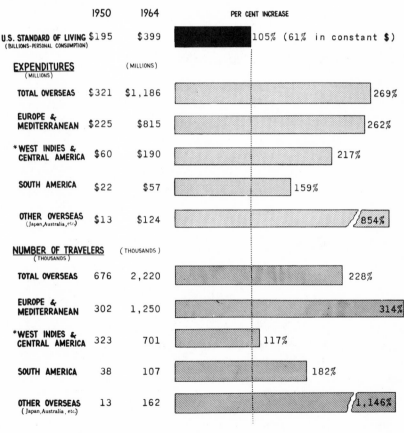

	1950	1964	PER CENT INCREASE
U.S. STANDARD OF LIVING (BILLIONS-PERSONAL CONSUMPTION)	$195	$399	105% (61% in constant $)
EXPENDITURES (MILLIONS)		(MILLIONS)	
TOTAL OVERSEAS	$321	$1,186	269%
EUROPE & MEDITERRANEAN	$225	$815	262%
***WEST INDIES & CENTRAL AMERICA**	$60	$190	217%
SOUTH AMERICA	$22	$57	159%
OTHER OVERSEAS (Japan, Australia, etc.)	$13	$124	854%
NUMBER OF TRAVELERS (THOUSANDS)		(THOUSANDS)	
TOTAL OVERSEAS	676	2,220	228%
EUROPE & MEDITERRANEAN	302	1,250	314%
***WEST INDIES & CENTRAL AMERICA**	323	701	117%
SOUTH AMERICA	38	107	182%
OTHER OVERSEAS (Japan, Australia, etc.)	13	162	1,146%

* INCLUDES BERMUDA - DOES NOT INCLUDE MEXICO, PUERTO RICO OR VIRGIN ISLANDS

Chart 31

$11 BILLION FOREIGN TRAVEL MARKET POSSIBLE IN 10 YEARS

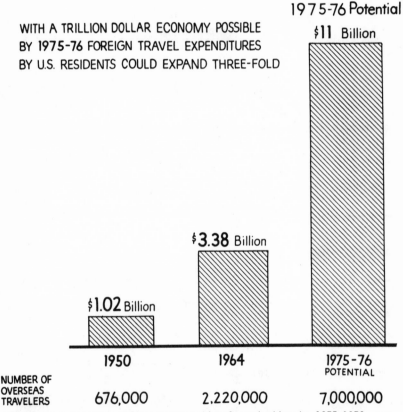

WITH A TRILLION DOLLAR ECONOMY POSSIBLE
BY 1975-76 FOREIGN TRAVEL EXPENDITURES
BY U.S. RESIDENTS COULD EXPAND THREE-FOLD

1975-76 Potential
$11 Billion

$3.38 Billion

$1.02 Billion

	1950	1964	1975-76 POTENTIAL
NUMBER OF OVERSEAS TRAVELERS	676,000	2,220,000	7,000,000

With over a trillion dollar gross national production by 1975-1976, our
standard of living or personal consumption expenditures should expand
over 60% - foreign travel is growing 3-3/4 times as fast as total real
standard of living (1950-1964 personal consumption in constant dollars
up 61% versus number of overseas travelers up 228%).

J. WALTER THOMPSON COMPANY

Change in Living Standards and Growth
of Communication and Advertising

The velocity of change in living habits in the United States since 1940 has been startling. For the period from 1865 to 1965, 84 percent of the growth in personal consumption expenditures representing the total standard of living took place in the 25 years after 1940. Only about 16 percent of the growth occurred in the first 75 years (*See* Chart No. 32).

This rapid improvement in living standards of the last 25 years has been coincident with the growth of communication and advertising influence: 86 percent of the growth of advertising has occurred during these 25 years while the 75 years before accounted for only 14 percent of the growth.

This has real significance in indicating the economic importance of advertising since the United States population during the past 25 years has grown only 39 percent. Sixty-one percent of the 100-year population growth occurred during the first 75 years, which represented only 16 percent of the growth in consumption expenditures and only 14 percent of advertising growth. Even if the consumption figures are corrected to a constant dollar, in terms of 1964 prices, we still must realize that 63 percent of the growth in physical volume of consumption has occurred during the last quarter-century with only 37 percent taking place in the previous 75 years, accounting for 61 percent of our population growth.

Particularly in the United States, Western Europe,

Chart 32

IMPACT OF ADVERTISING GROWTH

86% OF GROWTH HAS OCCURRED SINCE 1940– ONLY 14% IN FIRST 75 YEARS OF THE CENTURY

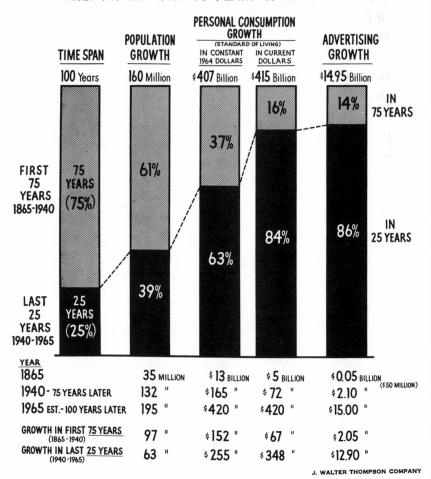

	TIME SPAN	POPULATION GROWTH	PERSONAL CONSUMPTION GROWTH (STANDARD OF LIVING)		ADVERTISING GROWTH	
			IN CONSTANT 1964 DOLLARS	IN CURRENT DOLLARS		
	100 Years	160 Million	$407 Billion	$415 Billion	$14.95 Billion	
FIRST 75 YEARS 1865-1940	75 YEARS (75%)	61%	37%	16%	14%	IN 75 YEARS
LAST 25 YEARS 1940-1965	25 YEARS (25%)	39%	63%	84%	86%	IN 25 YEARS

YEAR					
1865		35 MILLION	$13 BILLION	$5 BILLION	$0.05 BILLION ($50 MILLION)
1940 - 75 YEARS LATER		132 "	$165 "	$72 "	$2.10 "
1965 EST.- 100 YEARS LATER		195 "	$420 "	$420 "	$15.00 "
GROWTH IN FIRST 75 YEARS (1865-1940)		97 "	$152 "	$67 "	$2.05 "
GROWTH IN LAST 25 YEARS (1940-1965)		63 "	$255 "	$348 "	$12.90 "

and Japan, the rapid expansion of productive capacity expected in the next decade will force attention on the expansion of markets and upgrading of living standards through the educational force of advertising.

The Role of Advertising in Improving Living Standards

A new concept of advertising as an economic force is becoming apparent in the enlightened free nations of the world — those nations which are striving for rapid economic growth, full employment, and improved living standards.

This concept centers around the growing recognition that advertising of specific products and service becomes a *powerful and dynamic force in economic growth* — and that the expansion of markets through encouragement of a better standard of living is *in the public interest*.

With the growth in productive ability and the need for expanded demand to utilize expanded production potential, there has been a rapid increase in competitive efforts to upgrade consumer habits and likes. There is an increasing recognition of the educational value and sales stimulus of advertising. As people begin to earn more through increased productivity they do not automatically accept the standard of living concepts of those already in the better-income groups. There is a "Habit Lag" based on past training and experience. Advertising is a powerful force in overcoming or shortening this "Habit Lag."

The increased expenditures for advertising since 1940 are illustrated in Chart No. 33. In ten years, from

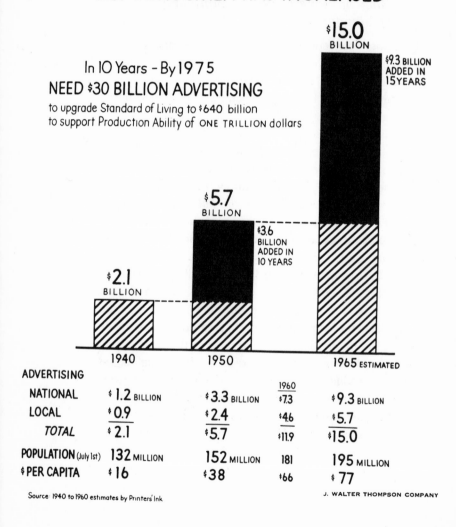

Chart 33
COMPETITION
HOW TOTAL ADVERTISING INFLUENCE ON THE U.S. CONSUMER HAS INCREASED

$15.0 BILLION

$9.3 BILLION ADDED IN 15 YEARS

In 10 Years – By 1975
NEED $30 BILLION ADVERTISING
to upgrade Standard of Living to $640 billion
to support Production Ability of ONE TRILLION dollars

$5.7 BILLION

$3.6 BILLION ADDED IN 10 YEARS

$2.1 BILLION

	1940	1950	1960	1965 ESTIMATED
ADVERTISING				
NATIONAL	$ 1.2 BILLION	$ 3.3 BILLION	$7.3	$ 9.3 BILLION
LOCAL	$ 0.9	$ 2.4	$4.6	$ 5.7
TOTAL	$ 2.1	$ 5.7	$11.9	$15.0
POPULATION (July 1st)	132 MILLION	152 MILLION	181	195 MILLION
$ PER CAPITA	$ 16	$ 38	$66	$ 77

Source: 1940 to 1960 estimates by Printers' Ink

J. WALTER THOMPSON COMPANY

1940 to 1950, total advertising influence directed to consumers grew by $3.6 billion from $2.1 to $5.7 billion (these figures include both national and local advertising). Then, from 1950 to estimated 1965, another $9.3 billion of advertising influence on the consumer has been added — an increase of 163 percent to an estimated $15.0 billion. That is over seven times the prewar total!

Maintaining adequate markets for the potential trillion-dollar level of production in 1975 could well require an expenditure of $30 billion for advertising, or twice the 1965 estimate.

Planning for a Decade of Progress

In summary, there appear to be some basic pressures and dynamic trends in the United States which point to opportunities for accelerated economic growth and upgraded living standards in the decade ahead — trends which marketing men should watch for possible worldwide significance.

In most of the free nations of the world there has developed, since the end of World War II, an urgent drive to increase production and per capita productivity. It is recognized that this is the basis for increased incomes and a better standard of living for all people.

Now, too, there is a growing recognition that markets must be developed rapidly enough to match these production goals and that private initiative and expansion of private consumption — through rapidly upgraded living standards — must be encouraged. This means vigorous and efficient expansion of marketing efforts and intelligent application of the educational force and creative stimulus of advertising.

In two areas alone which have been used as examples — the United States and Western Europe — the potential market for sales of consumer goods and services should expand from present levels of about $700 billion to about $1,100 billion by 1975–1976.

And this potential growth in consumer demand could stimulate correspondingly rapid increases in these markets for industrial goods and for world trade. Add to this the potential growth in production and living standards in Latin America and Canada, free Asia and Africa, and it can be seen that growth of world markets and the improvement of living standards in this next decade could be dramatic. I believe this worldwide improvement in living standards is the environment that will set the framework of American markets in 1975.

THE CHANGING INTERNATIONAL MARKET AND ITS CHALLENGES TO THE UNITED STATES

by Gilbert E Jones

PRESIDENT

IBM WORLD TRADE CORPORATION

Introduction

Obviously, I am not a professor but rather a salesman, and I am speaking to you as an individual, deeply interested in our international marketplace. Literally my entire working career has been connected with the IBM Company, which by almost any standard would be considered a large company. Undoubtedly you will find me biased in my approach to my subject because of this connection.

IBM has a slogan: "World Peace Through World Trade." I well remember during World War II, looking up at our building at 590 Madison Avenue with my Navy uniform on and pondering the practicality of that slogan. Yet IBM has tried continually to live up to this motto. It feels strongly that the best ambassadors of the American way of life are its international industries. What is a more forceful sales tool for democracy than a successful demonstration of our capitalist system in action?

My subject deals with the importance of the international market, the challenges that this marketplace presents and the various ways available to American business, through its penetration of the foreign industrial structure, to enhance our economy.

The Revolutions Taking Place around Us

The world is changing at a rate of acceleration that is drastically affecting our rapidly shrinking world. This rate is not a straight line on a chart; it is a steep curve affecting practically every area of our lives.

The population explosion is a good example. At the birth of Christ the world's population was doubling approximately every 1,000 years. By 1500, it was doubling every 200 years. By 1860, it was doubling every 100 years. Today it is doubling every 40 years, and by 2000 it will be doubling every 20 years.

The same is true of transportation. Its pace has changed dramatically even in our lifetime. Our grandfathers used the "high speed" horse and carriage. Our fathers' childhood witnessed the birth of the "Tin Lizzy." In 1927 Charles Lindbergh spanned the Atlantic in thirty-three and one-half hours. By 1945 his time was shortened to fourteen hours. Today it is closer to five. By 1972 it will be two and one-half hours. Rockets are making it possible to shorten such times even further with speeds up to 20,000 miles per hour.

Manufacturing is also changing. The speed of the miracle manufacturing cycle that Henry Ford developed to produce the Model "A" compares rather unfavorably with the time it now takes to produce a Ford or Chevrolet. Five years from now this time will be substantially reduced by further automation.

And nowhere is revolutionary change more apparent than in the methods of processing data. In 1812, Charles Babbage designed but was unable to construct the first computer. By 1892, Herman Hollerith was using a mechanized punched card for tabulating the census. By 1915, we had numerical tabulators. By 1937, we had a collator and, therefore, a really sophisticated punched card installation.

Dr. J. P. Eckert and Dr. John Mauchly constructed the first real computer at the University of Pennsylvania around 1947. The name *Univac* became famous in 1949 or 1950. In 1951, IBM began production of a few IBM 701's and IBM 702's. Our first commercial electronic computer to be manufactured in volume, the IBM 650, was not installed until early 1954.

In the next ten years computers went from tubes to transistors to integrated circuits at a fantastic rate. Of all computers now installed, 85 percent have been built in the last five years. According to one industry estimate, the number of installed computers in the United States climbed from 810 in 1955 to 25,500 by last December. By that time, approximately 6,000 computers had been installed in Western Europe, and roughly 2,000 more had been put to work in other areas.

As the number of computers increased, so did the speed at which we process data. In the 1930's, we talked in terms of one hundred punched cards a minute. In the 1940's, we talked in terms of seconds. By 1956 computer speeds were measured in milliseconds, or one-thousandths of a second. By 1960 the criteria was microseconds, or one-millionths of a second. Today the measurement is often nanoseconds, or one-billionths of a second.

The rapid rate of change in our industry mirrors the fact that the physical sciences are on that same steep curve. Did you know that of all the physical scientists who have earned Ph.D. degrees, 91 percent are alive today? Ninety percent of what students studying for their doctorates in the physical sciences learn in today's universities was not known twenty years ago.

The process of transmitting information — in the spoken word, the written word, or as a picture — has increased in speed at the same rate as the development of computers. The Comsat satellites represent the latest commercial state of this aspect of the art of communications.

What do all of these facts suggest? *They suggest that these changes in population, transportation, automation, technology, communications are having a radical effect on the future shape of our business. They make it obvious that business has got to grow bigger. They make it obvious that competition has got to grow keener. And most important, they make it obvious that our businesses have got to grow increasingly international.*

Implementation of improved technology and automation is a costly affair. But only businesses which are large enough to bear this expense and to utilize the consequent speed, quality, and reliability of their production processes can remain successful in national and international competition.

Modern business must look to an ever-growing market to absorb increases in production. Part of this increase can come from its domestic market. Most of it must come from the relatively untapped international market. Only 4 percent of our Gross National Product represents exports overseas as compared to 14 percent in Britain and 22 percent in Sweden.

Overseas Markets: The Role of Governments

There are many considerations that affect efforts to expand business overseas, one of the most important of which is government here and abroad. Washington represents both a help and a hindrance. Without question the Administration's foreign aid program has been of tremendous assistance to the United States businessman abroad. Although we are of the opinion that it could stand better administration in some countries, it is a highly successful program. The very fact that the Communists copy us is evidence enough to me that we should continue, not curtail, aid.

I was amused during a recent trip to the Far East to hear General Carlos P. Romulo from the Philippines talk about aid. He drew a verbal picture of the inevitable: twenty-five Red demonstrators with their Red placards in front of an American Embassy yelling "Yankee Go Home!" He then told us that in most instances the demonstrators were paid by the Communists. This was done on the theory that American newsmen would cable pictures back home which would persuade citizens in Kansas, Utah, and Arizona to wire their Congressmen and call off the Aid Program, thereby reducing United States influence in overseas business communities.

The Administration is also particularly helpful in its continuing battle to lower tariffs. The results have been far from perfect, but our government has tended to take the lead for strong, free trade. We have hopes for the so-called Kennedy round at GATT, even though it appears bogged down at present. We believe that the best way to tap the international marketplace is to negotiate more reductions in tariffs.

Washington can be extremely helpful in expanding markets. The Administration is leaning towards a thaw in our trading attitude with the Communist world. Bear in mind that over one-third of the people in the world live within the Communist orbit.

Our controversial wheat deal with Russia was probably the first sign of this thaw. However, our Government's policy has continually been to assist those nations who demonstrate their ability to think and act independently of Moscow and Peking. First Yugoslavia, and now all Eastern European countries are getting more attention from the United States and other parts of the Western World.

Our Government is quite explicit on this point: It is interested in promoting free trade with Eastern Europe in peaceful goods, and it forbids any trade in strategic items. Its definition of strategic items includes anything that would assist an Eastern European country in a war effort. The Government also prohibits export of our latest scientific technologies.

Speaking as an individual, I am strongly opposed to

trade with Red China or with any country whose stated objective is to destroy the United States. However, I am in favor of trade with Eastern Europe, provided such trade conforms with the policy of our Government. I cannot understand why we should allow this emerging market to be eaten up by European competitors when it is to our best interest — both now and in the future — to expose these countries to American ways, American philosophies, and the American people.

In some ways our Government has not been so helpful. For example, its present policy on the balance of payments problem does not represent an incentive to build overseas markets. We recognize that the United States, as pointed out by our Administration, has a temporary problem concerning balance of payments. As a company, IBM is strongly supporting the President's program of voluntary restrictions. However, I hope it is a short, temporary program rather than a long-range one.

I believe foreign investments, by building plants and by supporting overseas marketing efforts, represent a capital gain, not a capital loss. I believe such investments will cause future trade surpluses to increase. By creating new demand for further export products, they should provide further support for our balance of payments position through increased profit remittances and interest. Such investments, if managed correctly, are the best ways to increase our international business.

Our Government also has a less than favorable viewpoint on the question of size. My thesis includes the necessity for *big* business as a means of keeping United States industry competitive.

The United States government, although recognizing the economic necessity for large business, favors certain limitations upon size and growth. Being, I suppose, a capitalist at heart, I would hope that bigness would be judged by its proficiency and its contribution to society, rather than being condemned merely for its size. Of course, if a company uses its size to overpower its competitor, we would all agree that it should be controlled. Likewise I do not mean to suggest that a company need be as large as General Motors Corporation to be successful. I am only implying that the trend in the next ten years will be towards larger companies than today, not smaller ones.

Looking at governments overseas, their tendency in the past ten years to form regional trading areas, such as the Common Market, EFTA, LAFTA and the Southeast Asian group, has enhanced the stability of the economic environment in many locations. The associated reduction of controls within these trading regions has been a boon to multi-national companies. Obviously, the bigger these trade areas become, the easier it is to work profitably in the marketplaces which they create.

On the negative side, there has been an ever-increasing trend towards economic nationalism. I will say more on this later, but briefly this trend is affecting, and will affect, international business more and more during the next five years. Governments are much more interested in protecting their national industries than ever before.

Economic nationalism has many aspects. At its worst, it is little more than a political football whose every toss results in daily newspaper articles. Probably the countries most deeply involved at the moment are England, France, and Japan. However, we are feeling the impact of the "Buy National" theme throughout the international marketplace.

Economic nationalism usually results in high tariffs and government restrictions. It also often results in a government decree to buy only national products (when available) for the public sector of the economy. In many cases it results in government aid for a national industry. For example, in IBM's industry right now, British and Japanese computer manufacturers are heavily subsidized by their governments. I should point out that this is nothing new to the United States. We are the greatest subsidizers in the world. Look back at our airline industry, at our shipping industry and, of course, at our farms.

Other government deterrents have very little to do with economic nationalism but are aimed at keeping a country strong. The United States Government's program of voluntary controls to balance payments is one example of this. Monetary control in Japan and price control in France are two examples of very powerful government controls which make it more difficult to do business in those countries.

Overseas Markets: Economic Conditions

There are some sheer economic considerations which should also be mentioned in our discussion of the international marketplace. An American financial writer once commented: "The European working classes work to eat, walk (or bike) to work, and represent no market for goods." However, in the ten-year period between 1953 and 1963 the private per capita consumption in the United States increased 18.3 percent, in Europe consumption increased 51.8 percent and in Japan consumption climbed an incredible 86.8 percent. Now these people take autos to work, and they represent the fastest growing consumer market in history.

It is well-known that the Gross National Product abroad in most cases is growing faster than it is here. Japan is a prime example. Although recovering from a recent recession resulting from industrial indigestion, her current 4.6 percent in GNP compares favorably with a boom year in the United States. Her forecast for the next few years would indicate a staggering 8 percent annual average increase.

Europe's need for goods, her relative monetary stability, and her drastic reductions in trade barriers through the EEC have all helped to lure capital and international trade. Her markets are still relatively untapped. Where we have roughly 350 cars per 1000 people, she has less than 100. Less than 50 percent of her homes have washing machines or refrigerators compared to 90 percent and 99 percent respectively in America. New technological fields such as color television are just beginning to open up. Looking at capital production machinery, European machine-tool expenditures have increased by 118 percent since 1955 compared to a United States increase of only 14 percent for the same decade. American investors are highly sensitive to these developments. United States investment in Europe is now $12 billion—a 360 percent increase over what it was ten years ago.

Wage rates and productivity are obvious economic considerations which play an important, if not decisive, role. Comparing wage rates overseas to ours, we find they are invariably lower—sometimes as low as one-third of ours, often only one-half of ours. However, these wage rates, particularly in the industrialized countries, are going up rapidly. As they do, they tend to enhance our ability to be competitive. They also tend to raise the standard of living. Our job is to keep a tight rein on inflationary forces by limiting wage increases to proportionate rises in productivity.

One of the strengths of our country is its lead in automation. Through automation we are able to increase our competitive position abroad despite differences in the cost of labor. However, the benefits of automation are dissipated by such restrictions as "make-work" and "feather-bedding." Communist countries will utilize automation wherever it enhances productivity. If the free world is to maintain its strengths, it will be necessary to do the same.

Lastly, when discussing economic considerations, the degree of business risk has obviously to be taken into account. Doing business in the fifty states is somewhat complicated by various state laws, but these complexities are mere nuisances compared to the legal and tax problems in the many countries outside our borders.

There are archaic laws which have to be considered. Socialism in certain countries makes the ground rules for hiring and firing personnel extremely difficult. Political instability and monetary devaluations are business risks to be measured. The possibility of expropriation and other government actions are ever-present. All these factors tend to discourage the development of new markets.

The excellent Report of the Advisory Committee on Private Enterprise in Foreign Aid addresses itself to some of these risks. It suggests ways that the Johnson Administration can assist in minimizing them. We hope our able President will be guided by this report.

Before launching our effort to penetrate the international marketplace of tomorrow, we should first comment briefly on two key factors: How our competition abroad is doing and what resources there are to combat economic nationalism.

Competition Abroad

First, let us discuss competition. If in the past foreign goods were correctly classified as inferior, they certainly are not today. By and large, they are excellent. Where overseas companies once lacked service facilities, today most of them have widespread and competent services. Japanese televisions, radios, and cameras, highly price-competitive, meet the requirements of our most particular buyers. The Volkswagen, a product representing a top example of a multi-national business headquartered abroad, has established itself as the traveling companion of our Fords and Chevrolets. Moreover, the company has built an outstanding American image for this auto through the ingenious ads of Doyle Dane Bernbach Inc. Their stress of service and insistence on performance is part of any American marketing success story. But the important point is that they are just one of many. The Rolls, Mercedes, and Jaguar have always appealed to a select group, but look at Volvo, Fiat, Peugeot, and a host of others competing in our most exclusive American market. An equally unusual example of foreign penetration is in the pharmaceutical field where the Swiss, despite a minute domestic market, have established a highly competitive role for themselves.

You may also have heard that our worker, our engineer, our salesman is more productive than his overseas counterpart. Although this may be true in some cases, IBM can prove just the opposite. There is an obvious effect of education, management, incentives, etc., but time after time in our business we have found that if you can equalize work conditions the overseas employee is equally productive.

The point is this: Any advantages that we have over our overseas competitors are small and, at best, temporary. Competition breeds progress. Others outside of the United States have learned this; they are beginning to foster competition. They also realize that bigness and world-volume markets are needed if they are to repulse the American invader at home. Mergers and the disappearance of the family company are becoming everyday occurrences. Anyone who pictures our typical overseas competitor as a small, backward company using windmills for power, sampans for transportation, or hand tools for production has quite a surprise in store for him.

Thus, to earn our share of the lucrative overseas market, we have to overcome all the unusual challenges of the United States marketplace: We must either have a demand or create one; we must develop and produce a quality product to meet that demand at a price which gives the customer at least the value he expects (hopefully a little more) and, in most cases, make provisions for quality service. But in addition, we have to develop a favorable rapport with our customer's national government. This is no easy matter in the face of growing economic nationalism. And on its successful accomplishment hangs a large percentage of our overseas penetration.

Combating Economic Nationalism

I can do no more than stress the importance of good relations with foreign governments and perhaps review briefly two or three approaches my company has used successfully. In so doing, I do not mean to imply that these methods will work for everyone, but they may indicate possible alternatives.

First, IBM manufactures 90 percent of its overseas products in fifteen factories located outside of the United States. To be sure, this involves drawbacks, from the point of view of the host country, such as losses of fees and royalties, dividends, and perhaps more competition for local companies. But there are also advantages which are extremely appealing. To begin with, the technological advantages of foreign-situated factories are available to people in the industry. In addition, indigenous companies which supply the factories grow and develop with greater sales. At our newest location in Bombay, India, we are already dealing with over two hundred Indian vendors for parts and materials. It is true that most of these vendors are small, but their growth does not go unnoticed by an Indian government anxious to develop a technical manufacturing capability.

The wages paid and the taxes collected, the exports generated and the imports saved — these are other tangible pluses to the overseas government. The contributions to charities, civic institutions, and other forms of social welfare are perhaps less tangible but nevertheless important.

United States investors in the future will gain even greater favor if they can successfully build in less congested areas overseas. Italians might object to a new American factory in Milan, but they would probably welcome the same plant in southern Italy or Sicily.

The emotional issue usually centers around the *impact* of foreign, i.e., American investment: Will the United States dominate our economy? In partial answer we can say that if an investment in bricks and mortar attracts more foreign investment, it also stimulates a growing economy.

The worst case against United States dominance through foreign investment can probably be made in Canada. There American investors owned roughly 40 percent of the investment pie in the 1940's and 50 percent in the 1950's; today they own 60 percent. Yet, in a biased sort of way, I agree with Lester Pearson, Canada's Prime Minister, who once said:

If we try to sing the "Star Spangled Banner" and moan about the Star Spangled Economy, I would only state that if the U.S. investment brings too much U.S. control of our economy it will be our own fault. U.S. firms must conform to Canada and Canadian law. The remedy is in our own hands.

In addition to building plants abroad, IBM has located many of its research and development facilities outside of the United States. The same logic applies to laboratories as it does to plants. However, there is another important factor from the point of view of the country involved: Establishing labs within the country itself helps to minimize the "brain-drain" objections often heard.

From IBM's side of the fence, our six overseas laboratories have several major advantages. They facilitate finding the topnotch engineers in scarce supply everywhere, and they make available a world-wide range of knowledge, ability, and ideas. For example, our recent family of System/360 computers had a large input of German, French, Swedish, and particularly British inventiveness.

Our development laboratories abroad also tend to make what is basically a marketing job — that of collecting world-wide product requirements — much easier. Engineers seem to communicate better than salesmen, at least across country borders.

The employment of nationals is imperative to combat the effects of economic nationalism. IBM, as well as almost all growing multi-national companies, practices this policy. But two additional points are important in this respect: First, it behooves all of us to "attempt" to be bi-lingual or even multi-lingual. I emphasize "attempt" because the intent is often more important than the degree of success. Secondly, a well-trained national, thoroughly familiar with his country and his countrymen, will produce more per dollar in less time than any number of well-intentioned Americans.

Perhaps the major interest an overseas government has in welcoming a company to its shores involves ownership. Companies owned entirely by outsiders are likely to be the first targets of "Buy National" attacks. Companies with minority outside holdings are among the last. Without question, national partners are desirable whenever possible, providing they do not impose limitations on effective management. It is paradoxical to me that the countries that have the least available capital are usually the ones who make the strongest demands for a majority national interest.

One approach in countering economic nationalism is the encouragement of foreign ownership in the multinational parent company. For example, IBM lists its stock on six foreign exchanges and invites employees in foreign subsidiaries to participate in discounted stock-purchase plans wherever such plans are legal. Foreign participation on multi-national boards of directors is another trend to be encouraged.

We certainly do not want to leave the impression that all it takes for an American to survive abroad is to pick his spot, hire nationals, adapt to local customs, and then sit back and watch the profits roll in. We have discussed two commanding challenges: competition and economic nationalism. It is our main thesis that to meet these challenges successfully in the next ten years we will have to export our major strengths. These strengths are three: our technology, our marketing prowess, and our management.

Exporting Technology

Earlier, we talked briefly of change. American ingenuity has had a lot to do with bringing about these fantastic changes. We are famous and hopefully will remain famous for our impatience with the present and our constant search for a new tomorrow. In our business, Mr. Thomas J. Watson, Jr., Chairman of IBM, constantly urges all of us to be "on a restless search for new ideas." That this is also true of our United States competition is dramatically demonstrated by looking overseas. Ten years ago, 82 percent of the non-IBM share of the data processing market was held by local companies. Today they hold less than 50 percent.

One reason for American technological excellence is our large investment in research and development. United States private industry has consistently spent more in this field than its counterparts overseas. Estimated in 1920 at $80 million, research and development spending in the United States grew 175 times in forty years to $14 billion in 1960. Current estimates place annual expenditures at $20 billion, equal to 3.35 percent of the United States Gross National Product. Research and development is the fastest growing segment of what has been called the "knowledge industry."

Research and development, incidentally, gives a handsome return on investment. An educated guess places

the resulting annual return in the United States at between 100 and 200 percent; in individual cases the figure
can be much higher. The classic example concerns research on hybrid corn in which the return was 700
percent. Even if these figures were less convincing, research and development would still be necessary in a
perilous and competitive world which depends on rapidly
advancing technology.

One key to international market penetration is our
willingness to export this technology. We should base our
future on our ability to keep ahead technologically.
Where we are the leader, we will always be welcome.
It is where we are behind and have little new to offer
that the doors of the marketplace will close and the
"Buy National" theme will succeed.

Technology works in our favor everywhere, even in
developing countries. I have to smile when I remember
how we first thought developing countries would welcome obsolete data-processing equipment as it was replaced elsewhere by new technology. Of course just the
opposite was true. Emerging nations, by and large, want
to jump into the twentieth century, not lag behind with
outdated concepts and devices.

The Importance of Marketing

Nevertheless, if you ask almost any executive what
makes American-based international firms successful, he
will not give credit first to technological superiority. He
will talk either about bigness or about marketing.

To Americans marketing is a recognized profession.

We are proud of it. The term "salesman" connotes a successful, well-educated American. Millions of dollars are spent each year on conventions and seminars honoring, entertaining, and teaching him new techniques. He gets credit for keeping our whole economy healthy. On his shoulders rests the major responsibility for keeping American factories humming.

This philosophy is almost non-existent overseas, although it is beginning to grow. In Japan our IBM salesman is ashamed of his title. In even the most industrialized countries of Western Europe, a salesman can seldom demonstrate his product to top executive echelons. The ability of United States executives to instill pride in the sales force by teaching marketing competence and the demonstrated results of our marketing prowess represent another tool for breaking international markets.

Good marketing connotes the ability to forecast market requirements and to launch a product designed for a broad spectrum of local needs. In the past, our willingness to export the right product has not always been outstanding. Big cars for narrow roads and giant refrigerators for apartment dwellers are two examples.

Edward A. McCreary tells some amusing marketing stories in his recent book, *The Americanization of Europe*. An American toothpaste company found that its appeal brought little response in Europe. There brushing is neither as frequent nor as furious as it is in America, and people simply do not feel guilty about not being able to "brush after every meal." Nor were the English particularly impressed when a ready-mix cake maker announced its arrival. As it happens, the English do not eat American-style cakes. The company retreated in 1963 after four years of valiant effort.

When IBM began manufacturing its electric typewriters in Europe, we found that they had to be redesigned. In the United States we use a 60-cycle motor; in Europe they use a 50-cycle motor which takes up more space. Later models were designed to accommodate both American and European-size motors.

My favorite example of the right way to market overseas is the way Sears Roebuck and Company has operated in Latin America. The company has successfully transplanted know-how in department store operations to local managers and employees. It has introduced extensive newspaper advertising of specials, and it has brought the revolutionary concept of "satisfaction or your money back" to its customers. Sears Roebuck has exported many American products to Latin America, but most of the time it has avoided direct competition with locally manufactured products. Rugs, furniture, and tools are three examples. Indeed, it has encouraged local manufacture first, by supplying a sales outlet (Sears), and second, by providing direct support in the form of financial, technical, and managerial assistance. It has also shown excellent marketing sense in adapting products to local demand. Bright colors and ultra-modern design in such items as furniture became the standards of Sears south of the border.

Dozens of other companies have been equally successful. They all point to an exportable American strength: our ability to market.

The Influence of Management

The last of our three strengths is management, the key to any successful enterprise. The remarkable effect of one good executive on a company has been demonstrated a thousand times; Mr. L. A. Townsend at Chrysler Corporation and Mr. J. C. Wilson at Xerox Corporation are two recent examples. The business policies of Mr. Alfred P. Sloan at General Motors Corporation and Mr. Thomas J. Watson at IBM are lasting illustrations of that investing maxim: "Show me good management and I'll show you where to invest your savings."

There are two principal assets of United States management worth bringing to bear on our efforts to expand overseas markets. Our first and greatest asset, surprisingly enough, is the high value we place on honesty and ethics. Regardless of what you sometimes read, American management places a maximum premium on differentiating between right and wrong, good and bad, honesty and dishonesty. In comparison with overseas business ethics, ours often shine, and it behooves us to continue to teach our foreign management associates that, if they want to be admitted as partners, our way of doing business is the first prerequisite. It is difficult to institute good cost controls in a country where many companies keep two sets of books, one for the tax collector and one for the partners. Likewise, business in some countries is a continual struggle to resist graft. Progress is slow but progress is sure; the influence of good American management is apparent in this regard.

The second asset is a result of our national appetite for business training. Six times as many young men and women attend universities here as abroad. In the United States we have over 175 advanced business schools and innumerable management magazines, associations, and seminars.

Until recently, Europe cherished the notion of management as a mystique and scorned business education. Change is now rapid. With help from multi-national corporations and United States universities, there are now business schools in Turkey, Italy, France, Switzerland, Spain, Mexico, and Pakistan. In addition, we have hundreds of overseas students in our business schools here, plus at least 4,000 students gaining eight to twelve weeks of practical training with businesses each summer.

IBM, like many multi-national companies, runs executive training centers, ours in Cuernavaca, Mexico, and Blaricum, Holland. In addition, we try to alleviate executive obsolescence through top executive seminars which range from one day to a week or two throughout the year.

And what of the men who are putting these managerial assets to work? Our penetration of the international market is managed by two distinct groups of people. First there are 25,000 American managers residing abroad augmented by many other Americans promoting American exports in every nook and cranny of the world. There was a time when these assignments were considered resting places for our aging elders or exiles to an economic Siberia. But today's manager is a highly qualified American who sets our image abroad. He is our number one ambassador. He must think of his job as a challenge to a successful future. He is a statesman, a general manager, an educator, and a salesman all rolled into one.

The second group is composed of non-Americans to whom we entrust our overseas future. These are people reared in an atmosphere vastly different from ours. Upward mobility in management overseas is not easy; avenues of promotion are blocked by rather fixed prerequisites which often discriminate against the more capable person. Heredity and educational degrees are the primary criteria in most countries. Others include seniority, formalities, rigid job descriptions, and strict adherence to organizational structure.

Moreover, slow decisions taken after long consultations and study are often the rule. The fear of error usually results in a fierce defense of the status quo. This contrasts with our love of quick decisions, consequent mistakes, followed by an even quicker reaction to correct the mistakes. One of my favorite quotations mirrors this American point of view: "A bad decision is better than no decision."

Our challenge, then, is to put our assets to work: To teach the strengths of our management approaches to foreign managers who, thus equipped, are every bit as smart, as aggressive, and as creative as we would like to think we are. We are fortunate to lead in scientific management approaches. Control reports as opposed to management reports, linear programming, PERT routines, management information systems — all these represent valuable technological exports.

Conclusion

History has proved that private industry pushes up standards of living much faster than does government action. Where industry is dynamic it can improve our lot in life despite government instability. Any visitor to São Paulo, Brazil, can attest to that.

With our leadership in technology, marketing, and management, American industry stands on the threshold of a wonderful ten-year expansion overseas. The opportunity facing our industrial society is unparalleled in history.

The real challenge rests on the shoulders of the multi-national companies. One hundred corporations hold one-half of United States assets abroad. The ability of our multi-national team to exploit American strengths will be the key to our position in 1975.

CONSUMER PATTERNS IN THE 1975 MARKET

by Darrell B. Lucas

PROFESSOR OF MARKETING AND CHAIRMAN
OF THE DEPARTMENT
NEW YORK UNIVERSITY

ARNO H. JOHNSON, well-known authority in business economics, and Gilbert E. Jones, international business leader, have projected some impressive probabilities for the American consumer in the next decade.[1] The future promises an increasing abundance of products and services, together with added leisure time and buying power to enjoy the prosperity. It is my job to take these vast potentials and to try to look at them through the eyes of the typical man, woman or child in the year 1975.

At exactly 4:00 P.M. today, on my way here, I telephoned the Equitable Life Office of Social Research and was told that at the moment of call the population of the United States was 195,603,056. This is a 1965 figure, and it may seem reckless for speakers in this series to treat estimates for 1975 with the same dignity as today's figures. But this is not so. The Equitable figure, like many 1965 estimates, *is an estimate* projected from

1   As described in the two previous papers published herein.

earlier known facts in the same way that a 1975 figure can be produced. Nobody made a new census of our population today. Equitable Life simply estimated by the same process used in making future estimates. In fact, this figure itself was once a future estimate; Equitable Life told me last November 16 the exact figure they would give me today. Perhaps, then, if we seem to imply some forecasts in this discussion, we can accord our numerical estimates much the same dignity, whether they are dated 1965 or 1975.

Considering the hazards of forecasting it is amazing how much of it there is. Two weeks ago, Arno Johnson provided us with projections which he prefers not to call forecasts. Ever since 1955 we have known that Peter Drucker could forecast 1975 adult populations and housing accurately because, as he pointed out, the people had already been born.[2] The housing estimates required his assumption that "romance is reliably constant" even though most people have not found it so. However, the important point is that there is a great deal of forecasting going on in areas which cannot be secured as tightly as the projections by Arno and Peter.

I go to my dentist and he tells me that I will have these teeth until I am eighty. I go to a faculty meeting and our Admissions Office tells us that there will be 2,650 students enrolled in the Graduate School of Business Administration in 1975. Two years ago, my distinguished psychology colleague, Dr. Gardner Murphy, supplied us with a lengthy article on "The Psychology

2   Peter F. Drucker, *America's Next Twenty Years* (New York: Harper & Brothers, 1955).

of 1975." [3] And, lest you think these men are overly bold, I remind you of our University President's televised discussion on August 29th, 1965, "University 2,000 A.D." [4] Just about everybody does some forecasting.

As we attempt to look ahead to consumer behavior in 1975, it would seem that there are four major subjects to consider:

1 We need to keep in mind the Production, Population, and Income projected in ten years.
2 Since substantial change is indicated for 1975, we should consider the Capacity of Consumers for Change.
3 Since behavior is closely correlated with attitudes, we need to give some attention to the Nature of Attitudes, and
4 Since many of the changes for 1975 are already in the making, we need to take a good look at Changing Conditions.

Examination of these four facets should provide a basis for a better look at the Consumer of the Future.

Production, Population, and Income in 1975

The two preceding lectures in this series have laid a solid foundation regarding future production, population,

3 Gardner Murphy, "The Psychology of 1975: an Extrapolation," *American Psychologist,* Volume 18 (November, 1963), pp. 689–695.
4 "University 2,000 A.D." discussion on the program, "21st Century: Threshold," broadcast by WNBC – TV (August 29, 1965).

and income. According to Mr. Johnson, our biggest figure — the Gross National Product — may leap from its current two-thirds of a trillion up to approximately a full trillion dollars in 1975 — measured by 1965 dollars! Along with this growth, consumer sales may increase from $425 billion in 1965 to $640 billion. Even more impressive is the expected growth of our total discretionary spending dollars — those dollars we do not *have* to spend — a growth which may raise the present $258 billion to almost double, or $460 billion. An 18 percent rise in our population, from 195 million to 231 million, may account for some of this, but obviously the greater part will have to be accounted for by changes in consumer patterns by 1975.

Trillions, billions, and millions are logically meaningful, but they may not be as comfortable or as convincing as the corresponding figures for family averages. Average incomes may go up from the present $9,170 to $11,300 (if I may continue to use Mr. Johnson's figures). Discretionary spending, in order to keep pace with family incomes and the economy, is due to rise from $4,500 in 1965 to $6,600 in 1975. These figures are all computed in 1965 dollars so inflation is not the explanation. Instead, the main factors are: some expected increase in what the consumer considers to be essential; and a pattern of buying and consuming which will account for most of the $2,100 margin. This is what I have come to talk about.

It would be a great mistake to look upon the United States as a self-contained market in which consumers will buy and live apart from the expanding world. I don't expect people from other planets to inject themselves into our consuming economy to any great extent by 1975.

President Johnson's first reaction after seeing our pictures of Mars, as you may recall, was relief that there were few signs of potential future invaders. There are economic challenges and opportunities, however, in future international developments, and these were made very clear by Gilbert E. Jones.

If time permitted, there are a great many points in Mr. Jones' talk which could be restated to advantage here. He has reminded us that world trade is the key to world peace, and that American business must grow increasingly international. The assets which he says will give us an advantage in world trade are our leadership in technology, in marketing, and in management. It is important for us to become increasingly bi-lingual or multi-lingual and, by promoting change in the multi-lingual markets of the globe, we will be able to quadruple our overseas business in the next ten years.

Mr. Jones also made observations which relate to consumer behavior in world markets. Nationalism works to keep our consumer products at a minimum in many countries. Any advantages our products may enjoy are exceedingly temporary, and we can no longer count on the superiority of American products. The private American per capita rate of consumption increased by 18.3 percent from 1953 to 1963, but the Japanese rate grew by an incredible 86.8 percent in the same decade. This, Mr. Jones stressed, is the fastest-growing consumer market in history. These and many other points in his talk will color the comments I wish to make about the prospects for the American consumer in 1975.

It seems a little staggering to contemplate the role

of the affluent American consumer ten years in advance, or even five years. There will be more dollars to spend and more goods and services to buy. There will have to be new consuming habits, new attitudes, and perhaps a whole new personal philosophy of spending. Before we get into the future psychology of the consumer, however, it may be helpful to glance briefly at the past and to specify some basic assumptions which are required for any forecast.

The most spectacular invasion of the family budget in the twentieth century was made by the automobile. Even Henry Ford, as he looked ahead, must have wondered where the average family could find money for a car. Woodrow Wilson, early in this century, may well have been influenced by Thorstein Veblen's theory of conspicuous consumption.[5] Wilson feared that the conspicuous luxury of driving an automobile would only serve to accentuate class-consciousness and resentment. Yet, today there are some 72,000,000 passenger automobiles in the United States; far in excess of the number of families. And the discretionary spending required by most families to sustain a car is not far short of the $2,100 increase Arno Johnson has projected for 1975.

The automobile is just one evidence of the capacity of American consumers to change their spending and living habits substantially. It required a generation to make the automobile an accepted budget item for every middle-income family that wanted a car. It does seem to give us a better perspective of the capacity of consumers

5   Thorstein Veblen, *The Theory of the Leisure Class* (New York: The Modern Library, published by Random House, 1934) pp. 68–101.

to change, and it should help us to view the spending of the consumer in 1975 with less trepidation.

There are some possibilities between now and 1975 which we must view with greater trepidation than the trials of consumers in an economy of growing abundance. For example, if we are to talk about projections for 1975, we must first charge off a number of shocks or stresses, as follows:

a   We must not only assume that there will be no major plague or pestilence to reduce populations, but also that the genius behind our wonder drugs will not discover a true fountain of youth that will perpetuate retirement.

b   We must assume, even as we pray, that there will be no nuclear world war.

c   It had been my intention also to stress the assumption that a sudden cessation of the cold war would not occur and throw our domestic economy into turmoil. I note, however, the recent report of a special panel to President Johnson, which stated: "Even general and complete disarmament would pose no insuperable problems; indeed, it would mainly afford opportunities for a better life for our citizens . . ."[6]

d   There may also be the implicit assumption that government will not find it increasingly necessary to hamper the tourist in his foreign spending.

6   John D. Pomfret, "U.S. Survey Finds no Economic Peril in Arms Cutback," *The New York Times,* September 6, 1965, p. 1. (Reference is made to a report of a Presidential Committee on the Economic Impact of Defense and Disarmament.)

e   And the final negative assumption is that employment and business optimism will not decline and that consumer spending will not stand still, in the years between now and 1975, and thus thwart the economic growth Arno Johnson has depicted for us.

As you may suspect, I will proceed with complete disregard of these negative possibilities; indeed, they are possibilities rather than probabilities. The economic projections to which the following discussion is geared have already been laid out before you. It is evident that the rate of individual consumption is not only expected to continue to grow, but it is expected to accelerate. An appropriate statement made by Don G. Mitchell, our 1961 Moskowitz lecturer, fits in here. He said "Today, progress is moving ahead exponentially; it is progress times progress, not progress *plus* progress." [7] Americans have already shown the capacity to increase consumption; now we are concerned with their capacity to multiply their rates of discretionary spending and consumption.

We cannot emphasize too strongly the importance of the consumer if President Johnson's pattern of prosperity is to continue. No one seems to doubt our production capacity, either for quantity or for invention and innovation. Emphasis upon the population explosion implies no doubts about our capacity to produce consumers. However, it takes a little over twenty years to produce an adult consumer, and we are addressing ourselves to

7   Don G. Mitchell, *The Challenges Facing Management* (New York: New York University Press, 1963) p. 39.

the next ten years. We are talking about the consumer responsibilities of Americans already born. Never was this impressed upon me so much as by the remark of a South Dakota ex-state senator and career farmer this past summer. He put it concisely: "Government has let me know that as a producer I am expendable; as a consumer I am *not!*" [8] The farmer, perhaps the last to surrender his claim to the role of cornerstone of our economic program, now sees himself cast in a more important role as consumer. Moreover, he must not only continue to consume; he must multiply his rate of consumption.

Consumers' Capacity to Change

Capacity to change; that is, capacity for variable response, is what psychologists say distinguishes man from all other animal forms. His wide range of sensitivity to environment and the unpredictable variety of his responses have usually confounded any attempt to put his behavior into a psychological formula. On the other hand, man often exhibits very rigid patterns of behavior and enormous inertia against change. Perhaps it is because cultural anthropologists have concentrated so much on underdeveloped communities and countries that they are able to cite endless examples of inflexibility. George M. Foster's book on traditional cultures is full of them. [9] In

8   The Honorable Lafe Lunder, ex-State Senator of South Dakota, privately communicated.
9   George M. Foster, *Traditional Cultures: and the Impact of Technological Change* (New York: Harper & Row, 1962).

fact, the specific cases are enough to make one wonder how our bumbling attempts at foreign aid have produced anything for us but hysteria and antagonism.

How, for example, can you introduce dairy cows and milk into communities where custom or religion dictates against eating milk or beef? How can you introduce automatic laundry equipment into homes where servants depend upon wash day for their social contacts with neighboring servants? How can you install American kitchen equipment in homes where the housewife is accustomed to a low hearth or a hearth in the center of the room? It may break her back if you require the cook to stand rather than lean or squat, and it will ruin her social life if a wall installation requires her to turn her back on friendly neighbors accustomed to using these hours for visiting.

Even the motivations for success and survival seem inadequate to produce rapid changes in certain cultures. Show the head of an extended Latin American family how to treble his annual income and he may merely yawn. Increased affluence for him means an ever-increasing group of relatives and others becoming attached to his family and to his pocketbook. Or, in another instance, offer to take a sick person to a hospital when he thinks of a hospital only as a place where people die. Such a simple thing as the introduction of running water can bring tragedy into a community, as where a leaky public tap starts a mudhole for breeding disease-carrying insects. Partial attempts at improvement may often prove harmful in the total context of a traditional living pattern. And fixed attitudes may greatly delay genuine improvement in situations where American know-how and dollars are eagerly waiting to do the job.

Nor are the resistant attitudes of backward populations unknown in our own culture. We still prefer the white egg in New York, though it is slighted if not banned in Boston. Whole communities held out against polio vaccine when the facts dictated otherwise. Isn't it a little amusing that New York City had to have water fluoridation administered to it rather than voted in? As a resident of the community of Upper Montclair, New Jersey, I feel a deep sympathy for a Berkeley, California, professor who complains that his community repeatedly votes down fluoridation. Ours has, too! Can the dental lobby be *that* powerful?

On the other hand, there are times when our American culture is expected to be a little too tolerant of customs brought from outside. I am reminded of the baseball incident late last summer when Giant pitcher Juan Marichal crashed his bat down on the head of the not-so-good Dodger, John Roseboro. A WOR news commentator chided us for being too harsh in judging a man who merely did what he would have done in his native surroundings. The baseball brass, however, concluded that Mr. Marichal was making excessive demands on acculturation, and levied an appropriate fine. Local police, with their usual hesitancy to interfere with crimes people have paid to see, maintained a complete hands-off policy.

Despite the above instances of cultural resistance, there are examples of great capacities for change, even on a national scale. Certainly the Japanese have demonstrated two spectacular stages of accelerated change.

They accomplished an industrial revolution in half a century, at a rate three or four times our own. This was before World War II. Since then their rate of industrial gain has been nothing short of phenomenal. The Japanese industrialist, like his West Germany counterpart, is willing to go anywhere to learn and then to imitate anyone who can show the way to make progress. When a management representative visits our shores, he asks not to hear presentations by people trained to think of his problems at home; instead, he begs to be told how we build a better industry here. He will make the adaptations.

The Japanese consumer emerged from World War II as a creature held back by custom and belief in Shinto. But Japanese consumers have, as Mr. Jones pointed out, shown more capacity than has their industry for accelerated change. The predominantly urban and universally literate population, despite continued consumer restraints by custom and by government, has developed a home life much like our own. In leading cities there are television receivers in roughly 90 percent of the homes. The refrigerator is small by our standards, but it is there, and it is big enough for their needs. And the Japanese family is permitted to buy an automobile if its small lot is large enough to park it. Remember, Japan is a small, crowded island. In the main, the Japanese consumer is as free as the attitudes of his group permit him to be. In that respect, he is not much different from most of us.

The Nature of Attitudes

Japan, West Germany, Sweden, the United States, and Canada have shown a great capacity for change in consumer behavior. Populations in some other parts of the world have exhibited much resistance to change. Changes in behavior reflect changes in related attitudes. Cultures have to be learned, but they are sustained by attitudes and habits hardy enough to persist. Often the behavior patterns are so well habituated that the individual is not conscious of the attitudes which underlie them. As an example, the American male may not realize that he treats women as socially superior, but I rather suspect the European male is perfectly aware that he places women in an inferior role.

There are, in addition to stubbornly held cultural attitudes, many attitudes held by individuals. Some of these are deeply rooted and are often the distinguishing traits of a personality. We enjoy socializing with the friendly, fun-loving, eternal optimist and we tend to avoid his counterpart. We watch the venturesome, self-indulgent free spender; and we often fail to realize that the likes of him have made our prosperous economy possible. Flexibility and adaptability are other traits which can make it possible to convert 1965 consumers into the responsive kinds needed for the economy of 1975.

Perhaps it is unfortunate that personalities just described are likely to be in the minority and that deeply held attitudes usually resist rather than encourage change. In fact, it must be obvious that attitudes are generally an obstacle to change and that all of the favorable attitudes have their opposites.

The most monumental evidence we have on the attitudes of American consumers is that accumulated and reported by Dr. George Katona, who recently honored the School of Commerce as one of its Ford Distinguished

Professors. Through surveys of authentic population samples, over nearly two decades, the Michigan Survey Research Center has built a continuous profile of consumer attitudes and behavior. As an example, they have found that the percentage of Americans who think installment buying is a good thing increased from 50 percent in the early 1950's to 60 percent in 1960.[10] While this may indicate growing acceptance of credit buying by the same consumers, it is likely that most of the change resulted from a ten-year progression in population in which conservative elders were replaced by less cautious successors to their own age groups. Many individuals stoutly resist all installment buying.

Not all attitudes are held tenaciously, and many attitudes respond quickly to circumstances. We get an unexpected salary increase, or we take a new job with a competing firm, or our daughter dances her way quickly onto the Broadway stage, and we are likely to adjust our attitudes accordingly. Even when the population seems to hold an attitude firmly, Dr. Katona has found in the marketplace, as in politics, there may be a great many people changing one way only to be offset by the changes of others.[11] On the other hand, when the total consumer population shifts on a deeply rooted attitude there will be many who change not at all. This will give comfort to those of you who think your own attitudes reflect stability and integrity, that it is only the public which is fickle.

10   George Katona, *The Mass Consumption Society* (New York: McGraw-Hill, 1964) p. 233.
11   George Katona, *The Powerful Consumer* (New York: McGraw-Hill, 1960) p. 73.

Optimism, as related to buying expectations, is an attitude which can change rapidly in response to circumstances. During the 1950's, Dr. Katona found there were times when new prosperity brought increased consumer optimism and other times when the loss of jobs by some people produced general pessimism. Continued increases in prosperity, such as President Johnson's administration has enjoyed, can sustain optimism. However, if prosperity remains constant, Dr. Katona has found that optimism tends to wane, and this presents quite a challenge to our leaders, both business and political.[12]

This all-too-brief discussion of the nature of attitudes may offer some hint as to how the public mind will work as we enter a new consumer era. Observation of other cultures would indicate that many populations are slow, but that others are quick to change consumer attitudes and behavior. There is even evidence of a capacity to accelerate change in some countries, including our own. On the other hand, attitudes are largely habits, and habits naturally resist change. I feel sure that millions of cautious 1965 consumers will carry their conservative spending and consuming habits on to 1975. If we had to market the 1975 total consumer product in the 1965 environment, it is doubtful that it could be done. Fortunately, we don't anticipate a constant environment, and we have ten years in which to make the adjustment.

12   *Ibid.,* p. 48.

A Look at Changing Conditions

Even from this vantage point, ten years away, we can clearly identify several important changes in environment expected by 1975. One of the most obvious expectations is an increase in leisure time as the result of a shortened work week. There are those who already forecast a 20-hour work week by 1975 and, even if that estimate is five to eight hours too low, the impact on consumer expenditures should be striking. We must assume, of course, that added income will accompany the shorter week, and that overtime or moonlighting will not fill up the free time. Leisure time and fat family budgets automatically suggest more spending. Diversions which involve the whole family and which require expensive equipment offer a prospect of major spending to promote group activities. It is never hard for the younger crop to find ways of increased spending.

Everyone cannot be expected to react to shorter work weeks in the same way. We still think of the top executive who *got there and stays there* through long hours of work each day, often seven days a week. Yet, a review of past experience will show that even this pattern can be changed. There was a time when our New York University student groups could invite and get a majority of the leaders of a particular industry to attend a Friday evening function. One reason for the response was that these distinguished members of our community were planning to spend Saturday morning in their offices. Today, the men who hold these jobs aren't even in town Friday evening; in fact, most are no longer available after noon on Friday. It seems probable that nearly all employed people can learn to accept a shorter work week. And this means a greater market for products and services related to leisure activities.

By 1975, family spending will be accelerating faster than the growth of incomes. The expansion of installment buying, use of credit cards, payroll deduction plans, and gradual conversion of constitutional cash customers, will facilitate a faster pace of consumer buying. Computerized systems for establishing credit and more moderate charges for extended payment plans may further encourage the consumer in making up his mind to spend.

Dun & Bradstreet is now centralizing its computer-adapted credit reporting on more than a million business organizations, for quick reporting almost anywhere in the country. It is not hard to envision similar credit facilities for 70 million families by 1975. By then, if the head of a family makes a long-distance call to a bank to finance a new home a thousand miles away, the bank may ascertain his credit rating faster than they can put the right officer on the telephone.

The changes in retail facilities defy guesses ten years in advance, although a quick look at California is often helpful. We have seen new techniques come and go in less than a decade. The impressive discount house gained its greatest advantage and then became almost indistinguishable within a comparatively short span. New concepts of shopping centers have achieved immediate success only to become obsolete in short order. The prospect of substantial automation of store operations cannot be overlooked. Already in Wiesbaden, West Germany, the labor shortage has encouraged development of automatic shopping. Mechanical vending should encourage increased buying both because people have longer hours of access to the store and because pilfering has to be replaced by purchasing. In our own retail operations we have yet to see the full possibilities of telephone shopping, professional shopping services, and mail order.

A realignment of buying power along demographic lines is a major consideration in predicting increased consumer spending. A current issue of *Look* magazine makes all youngsters look like decision-makers in the market.[13] The range extends from pre-teeners on allowances to schoolboys who make more than a thousand dollars during the summer — and spend it!

From other sources we learn of the expanded force of working women, who have always been good spenders, especially while single. And, if *the new pill* makes the lady more employable by reducing the risks associated with romance and matrimony, this could add up to a great increase in female expenditures in the next ten years. And as for the employed housewife, Neil DuBois, Vice President in charge of research at Foote, Cone and Belding, has pointed out, "The mature U.S. working wife not only has the vote and the job; she also has cash of her own, not doled out by a miserly male but earned and owned by herself."[14] The housewife, fortified with an independent

13   Gereon Zimmermann, "Kids and Money," *Look,* November 2, 1965, pp. 49 and 50.
14   Charles Sievert, "Sievert's Alley," *New York World-Telegram and The Sun,* June 22, 1965.

source of cash, can be counted on to be a significantly better spender.

Nor should we neglect the retired population with its growing buying power, health protection and living facilities. California's leisure town east of San Francisco and such communities as Rancho Bernardo, near Escondido, offer attractions for spending time and money and for protection while doing so. Children, retired people and the increasingly independent modern woman should carry a good share of the increased consumer buying needed for our economy in 1975.

Still another factor in the future economy is the likely increase in government services. If Medicare is to be followed by more socialization of medicine and if any important utilities are furnished or become more heavily subsidized by government, the patronage of these facilities is certain to increase rapidly. Perhaps the purification of air and an increased supply of clean water will be added utilities by 1975. Tax dollars, rather than discretionary income, would pay the added costs, although consumer expenditures can also be increased by tax supported governmental programs.

An example of how taxation can encourage consumer spending, even while reducing consumer funds, is found in our system of heavy inheritance taxes. As the tendency to confiscate legacies grows, there is more incentive to spend accumulated wealth and to pass on a smaller portion to heirs. The willingness of increasing numbers of men at the height of productive careers to turn to Universities for the more modest rewards of teaching can be partly explained by graduated income taxes and high inheritance taxes.

The new anti-poverty program is another example where tax money is to be redistributed with some anticipated effect on buying totals. It is likely, however, that this impact will be gradual and limited. Let's look in another direction. What about the promise of free tuition all the way through four or more years of college? Peter Drucker told us ten years ago that "No matter how good our planning, the financial needs of higher education over the next two decades [until 1975] cannot be met with the resources now available or in sight — including student fees, gifts from individuals, corporations, and foundations, and state or city taxes." [15] If the 12 million that Dr. Drucker anticipates are attending college in 1975, the government will surely play an increased role. The Higher Education Act of 1965, signed by the President this November 8th, is a major step in that direction.

A great increase in communications by 1975 could have enormous impact on the consumer. Television, enlarged through satellite systems, can reach the world — *could* reach the world if language were not such a barrier! But language and social barriers may be expected to exert decreasing restraint on communication, with a resultant exchange of ideas, reduction of racial and social barriers, and general acculturation as the size of the globe continues to shrink.

With a communications system capable of carrying sight and sound to all parts of the world simultaneously, there will have to be more efforts toward a common basis

15   Drucker, op. cit., p. 65.

for understanding. You will notice that I did not say a common language. If a single country — India — has fourteen officially recognized major languages, we cannot expect the miracle of a unified world language in a decade. We are more likely to have sight and sound combined in some standardized pattern easily learned by viewers of differing tongues. Perhaps this will satisfy Dr. S. I. Hayakawa's admonition that "We must bridge the language gap between all of these peoples [in 200 countries] before we have a real breakthrough in maintaining effective relations." [16]

There is another purpose in bringing the subject of communications into this context. Arno Johnson has urged the importance of a doubled expenditure for advertising in this country by 1975. If, during a decade in which population is anticipating less than a 20 percent increase, the advertising barrage is to increase by 100 percent, what protection can there be for the defenseless consumer? Let me answer that immediately by saying that you can't turn off your minds. Even though highly intelligent people have boasted that they do so, it is largely fallacious. If you turn for help elsewhere, you may grasp at the highway beautification bill, but that affects less than one percent of current advertising. You may also take comfort in new cigarette warnings on packages and the industry code on cigarette advertising. Right now you can't hope for early introduction of noncommercial network pay-TV since California voters have put its

16 S. I. Hayakawa, in a talk on "Crucial Questions in Speech-Communication Research" before the conference on "Frontiers in Experimental Speech-Communication Research" at Syracuse University, June 29, 1965.

chief backers into bankruptcy. A negative view finds little promise that we can abolish advertising or soften its impact.

On the positive side what, if anything, can be said in favor of increasing the present advertising tonnage (an industry term which some of you may think appropriate)? I think there are two important answers, and I will rejoice with all of you if obnoxious advertising can be reduced in the process. Our first consideration is that there will be more goods to buy and more time for advertising exposure in the next decade than now. We will need more information for consumers and quicker responses by them. Advertising, both persuasive and informative, will be needed to make marketing efficient.

The other consideration is something which could haunt all businessmen as the ratio of discretionary spending in the marketplace increases. *People don't have to make discretionary purchases.* They can postpone such purchases with little or no hardship. Dr. Katona found, during a recent recession, that people had the money for expensive durable products but were annoyed by the conviction that prices were going up unreasonably fast.[17] Even though they expected to have to pay higher prices later on, consumers chose to postpone the purchase of durables. Suppose the future consumer gets the idea that discretionary products and services are being priced too high. What, other than an intelligent advertising program, can enable the manufacturer to correct false impressions of price and to keep his brand at a high prefer-

17   Katona, *The Powerful Consumer,* p. 28.

ence level in the consumer's mind? Only a *seller's* market
can let up on advertising, and the prospect of the immediate future is not a seller's market, but a consumer's
market. Advertise we must!

Let me pause to put in my commercial here. I have
said we must advertise. I should add, "We must promote."
To that, I should add, "We must market in the fullest
sense." We have been talking about the capacities of
consumers to meet a future challenge; their psychological
adaptability to changed consumer patterns and increased
consumption ten years from now. These are capacities,
not going mechanisms which will take care of themselves. Consumers do not seek out and adopt new patterns. They merely present the potential, and only wise
manufacturing and dynamic marketing can enable them
to realize their full consuming potential. Believe me, few
sets of teeth would be brushed in the morning, few
mouths would be freshly guarded against bad breath,
and few daily showers would have the double guarantee
of deodorizing soap, if enterprising manufacturers had
not developed products and spent millions of marketing
dollars teaching an American population these socially
attractive habits. That ends my commercial and explains,
I hope, why there can never be an end to commercials.

We have rambled a good deal and have touched
upon only a few of the changing conditions in which the
1975 American consumer may find himself. Many important factors, perhaps obvious ones, have been missed in
our hurry to get to the role of the individual consumer in
1975.

The Consumer in 1975

Some of the attractions surrounding the consumer of 1975 would surely be a surprise to us now. There will be many products and services not yet thought of or invented. Even the developments promised ten years in advance can be exciting. The *Journal-American* hints at homes equipped with glowing wall panels for illumination, and typewriterlike consoles in homes for communication through a central computer utility by 1985.[18] New plastics for furniture and building, artificial fibers for clothing, and synthetic foods, which they forecast in two decades, may likely be well developed by 1975. Men should be making trips to- the moon and perhaps be bringing back a few souvenirs. But most of the stepped-up consumer travel will probably be closer to the earth's surface, even though at supersonic speeds. Travel will be faster, cheaper and more convenient. Incidentally, lest you underrate the significance of air travel, you might consider the fact that airlines spend fifteen times as much on advertising in the United States as either railroads or bus lines, and eight times as much as ship lines.[19] Just project the impact of this level of promotion on air travel in ten more years!

People will be better educated in 1975 than now. As

18   "Your World 20 years from Today," *New York Journal-American,* November 7, 1965, p 20L (from the Los Angeles Times-Washington Post News Service).

19   "1964 Advertising Expenditures of Major Public Carriers and Other Selected Travel Services in Measured Media Within the United States" (New York: press release of *Travel Research International*), New York, November 11, 1965, p. 7.

Dr. Hester has said, "College education should include cultural growth — new habits and appreciations." [20] This means that education will be much more than career training, and he suggests the invention of new degrees for returnees, which may tend to keep many people permanently matriculated in college. He also advocates the use of teaching machines, a trend which will discourage some of this audience and which will also attract consumer dollars for home study.

Arno Johnson depicts the 1975 consumer as an inveterate globe trotter, spending $11 billion in 1975 compared with only a little over $3 billion last year. Travel, like formal education, is an investment which defies one of the basic concepts of traditional economics. One trip to Europe by a native-born American does not satiate his desire for travel. Much of the tripled travel budget for 1975 will be spent not by homey folks who want one experience abroad, but by eager repeaters whose first trip led to a second, and then to a third with no end in sight.

This brings up a subject on which advertising and marketing men have long been at odds with traditional economists. New economic thinking has been introduced by John Galbraith, who proclaimed in an Arthur K. Salomon lecture in November 1965 that our intellectual debt is not to orthodoxy, but to heresy. It was in that vein that he stated in his earlier *Affluent Society*, "So long as the consumer adds new products — seeks variety rather than quantity — he may, like a museum, accumulate without diminishing the urgency of his wants." [21] Psy-

20   Hester, "University 2,000 A.D." See footnote 4.
21   John Kenneth Galbraith, *The Affluent Society* (Boston: Houghton Mifflin Company, 1958), p. 148.

chologists and marketing men will welcome this understanding, though it is a little hard to figure out why an economist has to go to a museum to find a suitable analogy for normal consumer behavior. The American tourist continually demonstrates the phenomenon of the insatiable consumer.

Foreign travel, it happens, is a matter of public concern, since it relates to our balance of payments. We were surprised when the late President Kennedy cooled our travel urge by cutting duty-free purchases to one-fifth. Now, according to Clare Boothe Luce in the November *McCall's,* President Johnson is hinting that if Americans do not "voluntarily cut down on continent hopping, they might find themselves faced, after 1966, with a stiff travel tax." [22] There are optimists among us, however. Socony-Mobil's chairman A. L. Nickerson told the American Marketing Association last June 15 that the balance of payments problem will cure itself in a few years.[23] He expects increased exports and profits from overseas investments to make up the difference. Mr. Jones indicated his agreement last week.

Regardless of the balance of payments problem the 1975 consumer is likely to find himself faced with an increasing governmental and public concern over what he buys and how much he spends. Dwight D. Eisenhower, in 1958, set a presidential precedent when he urged Americans to turn in the adequate old car and buy a new one in order to spur the economy. Thus we have

22   Clare Boothe Luce, in her monthly commentary in *McCall's* Magazine, November, 1965, p. 42.
23   A. L. Nickerson, "The Stake of U.S. Business in the Balance of Payments Program," a talk before the annual conference of the American Marketing Association, June 15, 1965.

examples of both positive and negative consumer instruction from the White House. States and communities have been much more articulate in urging consumer support of home industry. The 1975 consumer is likely to get more governmental advice on what and how to buy.

Public or popular pressures on the future consumer seem likely to increase also. There will surely be an increasing accent on the patriotic duty to consume. At the risk of criticism for using an extreme example, I think it appropriate to quote R. & S. Manley's comments, paraphrasing a story in 1954 by Frederik Pohl.[24]

"Pohl imagines a future in which industrial production has been entirely taken over by robots, while human beings — in order to keep the economic machinery going — are required only to consume. But consume they must. In this hypothetical society consumption has become obligatory; everyone has a quota — clothes, food, car, recreation, and the rest — and is severely penalized for failing to live up to it . . ."

As a matter of fact, the author designated a group of specially privileged selected citizens distinguished mainly by their exclusive right not to consume!

It seems much more likely and desirable for our future economy to be propelled by the attractions and excitement of the marketplace rather than by regimentation or a highly developed sense of duty to consume. Nevertheless, Pohl's is not a lone voice on this matter.

24 R. and S. Manley, *The Age of the Manager; A Treasury of Our Times* (New York: Macmillan, 1962), p. 429, referring to Frederik Pohl, "The Midas Plague," *Galaxy* magazine, 1954.

In September 1965, Russell Baker of the *New York Times* commented on the dangers of a philosophy favoring "a stitch in time." [25] According to Mr. Baker, what one man might save would only put eight others out of work. The consumer will continue to be king, but the patriotic consumer must continue to spend.

Finally, it should be emphasized that the 1975 consumer will be a much smarter buyer than his 1965 counterpart. Dr. Herbert A. Simon, one of our recent Ford Distinguished Professors, has some tantalizing theories about more intelligent satisfying.[26] If I may take a little liberty in interpreting Dr. Simon, the present-day consumer is too apt to decide to buy some product and then concentrate entirely on the advantages of one brand over another. Instead, it would make much more sense to keep a systematic accounting of each of our kinds of satisfactions, with a value attached to each. Then, within the limits of our funds, and with the aid of a mathematical model and a computer, we could do a much more scientific job of satisfying ourselves. Robert M. Hutchins, in a recent panel broadcast stressed the same point in a much broader context by pointing out that, with science making it possible to vary our living and social structure so enormously, it becomes all the more important to increase the educational program so that we can intelligently choose the most desirable alternatives.[27]

25   Russell Baker was interviewed on radio station WOR, New York at 8:30 A.M., September 3, 1965.

26   Herbert A. Simon, "Theories of Decision-Making in Economics and Behavioral Science," *The American Economic Review*, Vol. 49 (June 1959), pp. 253–283, especially p. 272.

27   Confirmed by letter from Dr. Robert M. Hutchins, president of The Center for the Study of Democratic Institutions, The Fund for the Republic, December 2, 1965.

This idea of optimizing our satisfactions offers a good closing note. Such a process should accelerate the spending of discretionary budgets in the future. We have already seen that consumers, while resistant to change, are capable of rapid changes in behavior. There can be no question but that changes already in the making — increased leisure time, income, education, and advertising — will stimulate the consumer to more spending. The environment of 1975, new products and services, ten years of learning to consume faster, and an increased popular acceptance of the key economic role of the consumer will undoubtedly enable him, under stimulation and guidance by a properly planned marketing program, to spend the extra 200 billion discretionary dollars which are expected to fall into his lap. Altogether, the factors which will make for greater spending, to use up the expected extra 2,100 dollars in the 1975 family budget, include the following:

a The 1975 family will include in its list of essentials or necessities many items now designated as luxuries.

b A larger share of the budget of dollars, as well as time, will go for both formal and informal education.

c Travel, and leisure time for it, can be expected to expand appreciably in the next ten years.

d It is inevitable that there will be exciting new products to tempt the 1975 consumer, and attractive, currently expensive products may be produced at much lower prices.

e Consuming-while-paying will become a more universally accepted basis for buying, and leasing may replace more outright buying. This will be a dual force, postponing expenditure of money on the one hand, while increasing buying activity on the other. It is assumed that the latter effect will exceed the former.

f   A continuing increase in the percentage of gainfully employed women will make women even more active in consumer markets.

g   Increasingly affluent teenagers, and graduation of the 1965 prodigal crop into adult market participation by 1975, should stimulate more consumer spending.

h   Poverty on the part of the destitute and the aged will be replaced by at least moderate sources of buying power.

i   Increased advertising and other promotional activity, per capita, will aid in moving products more quickly into consumer hands.

j   The consumer himself — or herself — will be a noticeably better qualified customer. He will know better how to get maximum values out of both his money and his time, seeking not only greater diversion and sensual satisfaction, but larger total reward in a philosophical sense.

A brief look at the rest of the consumer world for 1975 is by no means as encouraging. Billions of humans live in an environment which deprives them of material improvement, through poverty, illiteracy, a feudal system, lack of industrialization, class and governmental restrictions, unfavorable cultural and religious beliefs, social repression and a continuing population explosion. India, held back by illiteracy and a predominantly agricultural economy, finds its population growing at a rate which largely offsets the progress of continued five-year economic plans. Nearby Japan, already racing to overtake our own economy, lacks space and natural resources and, perhaps more seriously, continues to smother both domestic and foreign competition in its consumer markets. Competition, of course, implies salesmanship, an institution scorned not only in Japan, but in as celebrated a culture as France.

There can be rapid consumer gains only in countries having a strong middle class. Looking south, we find that Mexico has begun to produce a middle class through half a century of revolution, land reforms, and industrialization. How long it will take the rest of Latin America to develop a middle class with independent or discretionary buying power is hard to envision. There continues the threat of communism in Latin America, and communist countries have been notably slow in building prosperity or producing goods for consumer markets. Africa continues to represent a dubious area for consumer progress in the next decade, or in any early decade.

Already in 1965 the pattern of the American consumer is in striking contrast to the situation in other countries. Indeed, the prospects for 1975 are such that very few nations can be expected to gain on our consumer in the next decade. The prospects are actually for a growing consumption gap in relation to most of the world's population. The greater the gap, the more strongly nationalism will affect our business relations with retarded countries. Our own nationalism is almost certain to be whetted in 1975 as we prepare for our bicentennial in 1976. The only mitigating circumstance would be a worldwide trend away from nationalism. Perhaps, as we go about the business of enjoying the next decade of increasing plenty, we will find time and opportunities to help consumers in other countries achieve a greater abundance of their own.